A CENTURY OF
SUBMARINES

Jackie Fisher, First Sea Lord at the Admiralty, who dragged the Royal Navy kicking and screaming into the twentieth century. Although he regarded submarines principally as localised defensive weapons, he at least recognised their potential, unlike many of his contemporaries. His enemies, and there were many, scathingly dismissed submarines as 'Fisher's toys'.

A CENTURY OF SUBMARINES

Peter Lawrence

The nineteenth century meets the twentieth: 'C' class submarines alongside the ancient 'Admiral' class barbette ship HMS Camperdown, c.1908. From left to right: C8, C9 and C7.

First published in 2001
This edition published in 2009

The History Press
The Mill, Brimscombe Port
Stroud, Gloucestershire, GL5 2QG
www.thehistorypress.co.uk

British Library Cataloguing in Publication Data.
A catalogue record for this book is available from the British Library.

ISBN 978 0 7524 5477 1

Typesetting and origination by The History Press
Printed in Great Britain

Contents

Acknowledgements   6

Introduction   7

1.   Early Days   9

2.   War   31

3.   Between the Wars   59

4.   World War Two   87

5.   Today and Tomorrow   113

Acknowledgements

Several organisations and many individuals helped with this project, and thanks are due to numerous friends who provided advice, encouragement and beer. Without the ensuing hangovers this book would have been finished in half the time. Marie Blackman typed the text and failed to complain about my execrable handwriting; Pat Fitches supplied many of the photographs at a reasonable price and a few that were not; Brian Head gave valuable information on 'E' and 'K' boats; the late Gus Britton and the staff of the Royal Navy Submarine Museum made enjoyable the usually tedious task of archive research; and the late Karl Wahnig freely gave information and inspiration. Assistance also came from the public relations staff at BAE Systems, GKN Westland Helicopters, Fincantieri of Italy, and Howaldtswerke-Deutsche Werft of Germany. Like the little ship below, the above frequently came alongside when things got somewhat desperate. Any errors of fact are my responsibility alone and, if I have inadvertently breached copyright on any photograph, I apologise and hope it can be forgiven out of magnanimity for what this book aims to do. Lastly, to Marilyn, who puts up with a flat filled with books, photo albums and bits of helicopters, and to my daughter Imogen, who could say 'submarine' almost as soon as 'daddy' and who thinks submarines are 'cool', so long as they don't frighten the whales.

The submarine tender HMS Nettle.

Introduction

This book is not a definitive study of submarines. Do not, however, let that put you off buying it. It is a selective history in photographs, drawn largely from my own collection assembled over the last seventeen years, and my ambition has always been to make these images available to a wider audience. The obsession of many collectors with squirreling away photographs for their own private consumption has always struck me as rather sad. I have tried as much as possible to avoid using images from the more obvious sources such as museums and press agencies, partly because many have been seen before, and partly because I cannot afford the reproduction fees. The majority of the early photos are from contemporary commercially produced postcards or privately produced amateur 'snapshots'; the intention is to show both how the submarine developed as a machine and the nature of undersea warfare.

This latter aspect presents something of a problem as the photographic record is less than all-embracing, the camera lens less than all-seeing. A familiar cliché is that a picture is worth a thousand words and that a photograph, by freezing a brief moment of historical time, provides a 'window on the past'. Unfortunately, it is a very grubby window, the view through it often hazy and indistinct, and much remains out of sight. While the camera can capture the physical shape of the submarine, its attacks and the after effects, it fails to portray the unhealthy living conditions of the crew, the tension and fear as depth-charges come down or water floods a sinking hull. To understand that experience we need words: the memoirs and personal testimony of the men themselves. And that is how it should be.

I am an armchair submariner, but well aware that my admiration for these men runs the risk of lapsing into romantic mythologising. Despite attempting to maintain objective neutrality, I am continually struck by the widely held perception that submariners are a race apart from other naval seafarers. Viewed as heroes or villains subject to which side they are on (sometimes indeed regarded as villains by the senior officers of their own side), it is perhaps understandable that submariners have a reputation for independence of thought and action, and sheer downright bloody-mindedness. The nature of their job encourages these traits. They are faced by threats from hostile forces: both man-made and elemental. Safe operation relies on every crew member doing their job, and for a crew to work effectively as a team requires a considerable degree of trust, tolerance and mutual respect. Survival depends on it. Max Horton, arguably the greatest British submariner, once said with characteristic bluntness, 'There is no margin for mistakes in submarines, you are either alive or dead'.

It is a remarkable feature of human existence that former enemies, veterans of past wars, meet later in a spirit of reconciliation and friendship. This should give hope for the future, but these men grow older and time is on no-one's side. Those of us of a younger generation are then left with a void of lost knowledge and, by extension, lost understanding. The sudden death of my friend Karl Wahnig, a former U-boat crewman, brought home this painful reality. Yet the ancients believed a person never died if they were never forgotten. With that in mind, this book aims to be both testimony and tribute to the submariners of all nations, but is dedicated especially to the memory of those still missing; to those who are 'still on patrol'.

The Spanish Navy's Peral, *launched in 1888, and powered only by electric accumulators. She is preserved at Cartagena.*

The French Navy's Lutin, *a 'Farfardet' class boat, c.1905. Launched in 1903, Lutin was powered solely by batteries giving a submerged range of twenty-eight nautical miles. The four cylindrical basket structures on the casing are the Drzewiecke external torpedo launching cradles. Lutin sank with the loss of all fourteen crew during a diving demonstration in Lake Bizerta on 17 October 1906. Between 1900 and 1914, the French lost eleven submarines in accidents.*

One

Early Days

The submarine changed the surface of naval warfare, though at the beginning of the twentieth century it would have required a person of considerable imagination and foresight to have predicted this.

A 'Holland' under construction at Vickers' yard, Barrow-in-Furness. The small size of these boats is emphasised in this photo, which also illustrates the 'spindle-form' hull that led to a low buoyancy reserve and stability problems.

Holland 1 *under way in Haslar Creek with the Royal Navy's first submarine coxswain, Petty Officer William Waller, sitting on the hatch coaming while steering the boat.* Holland 1 *is now preserved at the Royal Navy Submarine Museum, Gosport.*

From the seventeenth century onwards, inventive minds had been attempting to develop submersible vessels. While many of their designs were theoretically sound they failed in practice – often with fatal consequences – principally due to the limited engineering knowledge of the times. These primitive submarines lacked suitable methods of propulsion, effective weapon, navigation and steering systems, and practical control mechanisms for diving and surfacing. None of this deterred people from continuing to experiment. During the American Civil War, in February 1864, the Confederates managed to attack and sink in Charleston harbour the Union sloop *Housatonic* using the submersible *H.L. Hunley*. The *Hunley*'s only armament was a crude spar-torpedo. This was simply a long pole protruding forward from the bow with an explosive charge attached to the far end. It was as dangerous to its own crew as it was to an enemy, and the *Hunley* went to the bottom with its victim. It was, however, a portent of things to come. The development of the self-propelling torpedo, the periscope, hydroplanes, and ballast tanks meant that most of the technical obstacles had been overcome by the end of the nineteenth century. Generating enough power to move a submarine a worthwhile distance remained the biggest hurdle. The *Hunley* had been powered by a hand-cranked screw, which rapidly exhausted the men operating it. Steam boilers worked fine while a boat was on the surface, but rapidly consumed the air inside the hull when dived. Compressed air also ran out too quickly. Electricity had potential, but batteries lacked sufficient capacity to drive the boat both on the surface and below. The solution was found by an Irish-American, John Holland, who employed a petrol engine for surface propulsion, leaving the electric motors free for submerged running. While the boat was surfaced, the petrol engine could also be used to recharge the batteries. Holland, a supporter of Irish independence, had originally intended to sell his design to the Fenians for use in their campaign against the English occupation. Instead, in 1900 he sold it to the US Navy.

Other countries, particularly France, Italy and Russia, were conducting parallel investigations during this period. The Germans, whose U-boats would later cause such carnage in two world wars, were, however, slow off the mark. As early as 1850 the Bavarian engineer Wilhelm Bauer had built a submersible. It sank on its first test dive, leaving German officialdom understandably sceptical as to the value of this type of vessel. Consequently, the first submarine was not commissioned into the Imperial German Navy until 1906.

At the beginning of the twentieth century the submarines under development were small, slow and of short range. These technical limitations inevitably imposed a restricted tactical role, principally to localised coastal and harbour defense, and encouraged the generally held opinion that the submarine was a weapon only fit for the economically and militarily weaker nation states. This prejudice was particularly strong in Britain, where the Royal Navy still ruled the world's oceans, and admirals still thought in terms of naval battles fought along the lines of Trafalgar. To many senior British officers the submarine was 'a treacherous knife dug in an opponent's back', captured submariners should be condemned as pirates and hanged. In short, the submarine was 'a damned un-English weapon', and serving in them was 'no occupation for a gentleman'.

Nevertheless, because other nations were experimenting with submarines, it was deemed prudent that the Royal Navy at least evaluate the ghastly contraption to assess what it might be up against. In 1900, the Admiralty contracted Vickers to build five 'Holland' class boats, *Holland 1* being launched in 1901. All five were in service by 1903, and the Royal Navy had its first submarines. Whether the British perceived the irony of purchasing a weapon originally intended by its designer to be used against themselves, by a section of their own population, is not known.

Although the 'Hollands' were armed with one torpedo tube and two re-loads, they could not really be considered practical offensive weapons. Due to the short and fat design of their hulls they were unstable fore and aft, which made them somewhat fickle in rough sea conditions, and prone to tuck their bows down and dive at the slightest opportunity. Despite these shortcomings, the 'Hollands' provided much valuable engineering and handling experience that benefited future design and operational developments. Considering that they were experimental boats, manned by crews with no previous experience of submarines, they were remarkably free of fatal accidents – unlike their successors.

The Imperial German Navy's first submarine, U1, c.1910. Launched in August 1906, and noticeably larger than the British 'Hollands', U1 was employed for trials and training purposes. It is now on display at the Deutsches Museum, Munich.

Holland 2 *alongside the depot ship* HMS Hazard *in 1904. The boat's weaponry of three 18in Whitehead torpedoes would be loaded - with considerable effort - through the open casing hatch.*

The 'Hollands' were followed quickly by the 'A', 'B' and 'C' classes. These were larger and slightly more sophisticated, but essentially variations on the same theme. They also had common design flaws that did little to improve safety or habitability. Their petrol engines were prone to explosive fires, petrol fumes caused dizziness, and trapped exhaust gases caused carbon monoxide poisoning. Most dangerous was the lack of internal dividing bulkheads, their absence allowing the entire boat to flood if the pressure hull suffered a serious rupture. Living conditions too were awful. The crew slept where they could, there were no washing facilities, and the lavatory ('heads' in naval parlance) was a bucket in full view. Not surprisingly, the atmosphere inside the early boats was vile: dank, fetid, and malodorous. All of this begs the question why anyone with a molecule of common sense would chose to serve in submarines. Yet there was never any shortage of volunteers.

The infant submarine service was derogatorily called 'The Trade', which says much about the snobbery that prevailed in the higher echelons of the Edwardian Royal Navy. It was like a mirror reflecting English society at large and, as one wit cynically remarked, the Navy existed principally to provide employment for the sons of the Royal Family and husbands for the daughters. Pre-war, promotion was determined not just by seniority, and still less by merit or ability, but rather by patronage. An ambitious officer did his chances of promotion little good by volunteering for submarines, given the antipathy felt towards them by many of high rank. Those who opted for submarines tended to be aggressive freethinkers, who foresaw the offensive potential of this new weapon system. They valued their independence and saw submarines as an escape route from the ossified, sycophantic social hierarchy that prevailed on the large surface warships. When at sea, they were free to use their own initiative. Petty officers and ratings possibly had similar motives, appreciating the relative informality and lack of 'bull', though in a navy where men were badly paid, the extra money for submarine service was also an inducement. All submariners, of whatever rank, also discovered their occupation made them particularly attractive to young women. Sadly, the same does not seem to apply to the authors of submarine books. At any rate, not this one.

Holland 5 off Gosport in 1905 with Cox'n Waller at the wheel. The tallest tube is the primitive periscope, held in place by wire stays, which was folded down onto the casing when not needed. The other pipes are ventilators providing much-needed fresh air to the crew, batteries and engine all crammed inside the tiny hull. Every such opening had to be sealed off before diving, and getting the boat under could take up to ten minutes. Because of their instability the 'Hollands' had to be driven at their full speed of six knots once submerged.

Holland 1, *with all but one of her crew on deck grabbing some fresh air while they can. The low freeboard due to the lack of reserve buoyancy is evident, and in anything other than calm sea conditions a prudent captain kept the hatch closed to avoid the risk of a wave swamping the boat.*

A SHOAL OF SUBMARINES ALONGSIDE HMS THAMES

Fisher's toys. Three 'Hollands' alongside the depot ship HMS Thames.

A1 in 1903. Originally laid down as a 'Holland', A1 was redesigned before launching and became the lead boat in the first British designed class. A1 also had the sad distinction of being the first Royal Navy submarine to be lost. In the Solent, on 18 March 1904, A1 was rammed by the liner Berwick Castle and sank with the loss of all eleven crew.

The funeral of the crew of A1 passing along 'Dead Man's Mile', the road from Haslar Hospital to Haslar Cemetery a scene that would be frequently repeated.

In Memory of

The following Officers and Men who lost their lives in the running down of the Submarine A1, on March 18th, 1904.

LIEUT. L. C. O. MANSERGH,
SUB-LIEUT. J. P. CHURCHILL,
WM. DUDGEON, P.O.,
G. G. BAKER, P.O.,
V. W. L. ROBERTS. P.O.
W. J. PARKINSON, E.R.A.,
C. FAILEY, E.R,A.
A. B. FLEMING, C.S.
P. S. WALLACE, A.B.,
C. W. KING, A.B.,
A. B, ELLIS, S.

Interred in Haslar Cemetery, April 19th, 1904.

An extract from an 'In Memoriam' card published shortly after the sinking of A1. The card also featured Tennyson's emotional poem 'Crossing the Bar'. These cards were regularly published in the aftermath of fatal British submarine accidents.

A3 alongside a depot ship at Portland, Dorset. The white bands around the conning tower were an experiment in signifying a boat's pennant number without using numerals.

British Submarine "A.3"

All fourteen crewmen died when A3 was hit by HMS Hazard during exercises off the Isle of Wight on 2 February 1912. Death stalks the history of submarines, and in the years to come, the phrase 'The Admiralty regrets...' became depressingly familiar to submariners and their families.

A5 in the Solent. At Queenstown on 16 February 1905 she suffered a devastating fire when petrol vapour exploded, killing seven men, including the boat's CO, and seriously injuring another twelve.

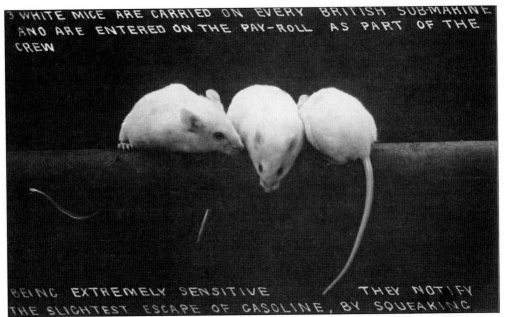

WHITE MICE ARE CARRIED ON EVERY BRITISH SUB-MARINE AND ARE ENTERED ON THE PAY-ROLL AS PART OF THE CREW

BEING EXTREMELY SENSITIVE THEY NOTIFY THE SLIGHTEST ESCAPE OF GASOLINE, BY SQUEAKING

Coal miners took canaries to work, submariners took mice. This was the Admiralty's solution to the danger of fuel vapours. Whether the mice were of any use is doubtful, but pet-loving sailors enjoyed their company.

The conning tower of A9, illustrating the rudimentary bridge structure. Conditions for bridge personnel were appalling in foul weather. Visible on the conning tower are ventilators and the single periscope. The small structure with two spheres aft of the conning tower is the binnacle, housing the magnetic compass which could not be kept within the confines of the all-steel hull: a feature also common to the 'Hollands', 'B', and early 'C' classes.

B1, c.1906. *The lead boat of the 'B' class, fitted with hydroplanes on the conning tower in an attempt to improve underwater handling. The idea was not pursued but the US Navy reintroduced it on their nuclear boats in the 1950s. The 'B' class took three minutes to dive, had a submerged range of fifty miles and an endurance of ten hours, running on the batteries alone.*

Crew members of a 'B' class boat wearing the improvised working rig of the average British submariner. A sight guaranteed to provoke apoplexy amongst the 'crushers' of the Regulating Branch.

'B' class boats alongside HMS Forth, with their crews looking their best for the photographer in spotless Admiralty-issue white polo neck jumpers. These, and a few sets of oilskins per boat, were the Admiralty's only concessions to ameliorating the dreadful conditions faced by the early submariners. Girlfriends, wives and mothers got their knitting needles clicking to compensate for the parsimony of the Admiralty bureaucrats. The 'A', 'B' and 'C' classes were, to put it mildly, inhospitable. Internal ballast tanks combined with the small size of these boats meant space inside the hull was extremely limited. Personal hygiene was virtually nonexistent as there were no washing facilities, and the toilet consisted of a solitary bucket to be shared by up to 15 men. If surfaced, the crew unburdened themselves over the side but, to maintain a degree of decorum, one needed to pay close attention to the direction from which the wind was blowing! For cooking, only a single hot plate was provided and there were no bunks, the men sleeping were they could. In wartime, if enemy activity forced a boat to stay submerged for any great length of time, the crew ran the risk of carbon dioxide poisoning, which could rapidly build to dangerous levels within the confines of the unventilated hull. Noise, fumes, dripping condensation, and damp unwashed clothes added to the general misery. Fortunately, the short range of the early boats meant they were rarely away from the comforts of their depot ships for any great length of time.

C1, lead boat of the largest British pre-war class. Thirty-eight were built and they served throughout the First World War. C1 survived and was scrapped in 1920. Of note is the exposed bridge with its lack of weather protection, and the two periscopes; one for the captain, one for the lookout.

C15 moored alongside the destroyer HMS Moy and the depot ship HMS Hazard during a courtesy visit to the Pool of London in July 1909.

C16 *underway. The canvas 'dodger' wrapped around the bridge provided the only weather protection for lookouts and the officer of the watch.* C16 *was sunk with all hands off Harwich on 16 April 1917 following a collision with the destroyer HMS Melampus.*

Sitting on the mud at low tide, C8 *conveniently shows off the shape of her 'spindle-form' hull of direct descent from the original 'Hollands'. Also visible are the bow caps of the two 18in torpedo tubes.*

MARINES,

HARWICH
HARBOUR.

'C' boats at Harwich in 1909. From left to right: C8, C9 and C5. In Hartlepool, five years later, Lt Deering would sail C9 out of the harbour and across the sand bars at low tide, in a courageous but unsuccessful attempt to get within torpedo range of German cruisers shelling the town.

H.M. SUBMARINE. C. 10.

C10 being kept well away from HMS Superb, the 'Bellerophon' class battleship in the background, to avoid disturbing the delicate sensibilities of the big-ship men.

The engine-room of C2. Although the 'C' class boats were larger than previous ones, living conditions remained primitive. The one amenity provided for the crew's bodily functions – a bucket – was usually situated here, presumably in the hope that engine smells would disguise human smells.

'C' class boats alongside the boy's training ship HMS Ganges, at Shotley, c.1910.

The French Pluviose after being salvaged. Pluviose was rammed and sunk by a cross-channel steamer off Calais on 26 May 1910. All twenty-seven crewmen died: the heaviest loss of life in a pre-war submarine accident.

C17 showing the revised style of the conning tower. Built by Chatham Dockyard, C17 was the first British submarine not to be built by Vickers.

THE ILLFATED SUBMARINE B2.
LOST OFF DOVER OCTᴿ 4ᵀᴴ 1912.

Failure to maintain an adequate lookout often carried a terrible price. Four miles off Dover, on the night of 4 October 1912, B2 was on the surface charging batteries when she was run down by the Hamburg America Line's SS Amerika. Though Lt R.I. Pulleyne was rescued, the other fifteen crewmen were killed.

A French 'Naide' class boat in the lock at Dunkirk. Two Drzewiecke torpedo cradles are fitted to the hull, an external launching system favoured by the French, but which prevented their boats from diving below 100 feet. Continual immersion in seawater did not do the torpedoes much good either.

Portugal's Espadarte, a Laurenti-Fiat type boat, launched in 1912.

D4 at Barrow, in 1911, shortly after commissioning. The 'D' class was a major technological step forward. They had diesel engines which were safer and more reliable than petrol; external ballast tanks which increased space inside the hull; wireless, twin propellers which increased maneuverability; an electric oven, and proper toilets. With a surface range of 2,500 nautical miles they were the first British boats capable of making overseas patrols. D4 also had a deck gun, soon to become a standard feature.

D7, c.1912. In February 1918, D7 would have a lucky escape when she was mistaken for a U-boat and depth-charged by the destroyer HMS Pelican. Fortunately, damage was minimal but such incidents, all too common in wartime, did not always end so well. Of the eight boats in the 'D' class, four would be sunk during the war from various causes.

SUBMARINES AT IMMINGHAM.

C4 of the 3rd Submarine Flotilla enters Immingham a year before the outbreak of war. The casing party are breaking out mooring lines, with the rating on the bow perched in a very exposed and precarious position. The extended casings of the later 'C's were safer places to work on.

Unsere Unterseeboote im Hafen.

U 11, 9, 6, 7, 8, 5, 14, 15, 12, 16, 18, 17, 13, 22, 20, 19, 21.

155

U-boats at Kiel in 1914. Of the seventeen boats visible, ten would be sunk during the forthcoming war.

U14, a 'Desiderata' boat, with units of the German Imperial Navy near Kiel, shortly before the war. Characteristic white exhaust smoke comes from her Körting paraffin engines, which were almost as dangerous as British petrol ones. Despite this, the Germans lost only one U-boat and three men before 1914, a tribute to their methodical training regimes and more rigorous design and construction methods.

Under the command of Otto Weddigen, U9, an antiquated paraffin 'Desiderata' boat with limited battery reserves, sank the armoured cruisers HMS Cressy, Hogue and Aboukir off the Belgium coast, on 22 September 1914. Three weeks later Weddigen struck again and sank the cruiser Hawke.

Two

War

War broke out in August 1914 and Britain's blasé assumptions about its naval supremacy were about to suffer a severe shaking. Though still a relatively weak force, Germany's U-boats would strike the first blows against a long cherished belief: the invincibility of Britannia's domination of the sea. In September, the cruiser HMS *Pathfinder* was sunk, followed seventeen days later by HMS *Cressy*, *Hogue* and *Aboukir*. All were old ships of little value, but the loss of life was appalling. Their sinking had a profound effect on the minds of senior British naval strategists, who became more fearful of submarines and more tactically cautious as a result.

HMS Aboukir in 1914. She had two identical sisters, Hogue and Cressy, and these three elderly ships made up Cruiser Force 'C', the 'Broad Fourteens' Patrol, which U9 wiped-out in the space of an hour.

Kapitänleutnant Otto Weddigen, 'The Polite Pirate', so-called by the British press because he never sank an unarmed merchant ship without warning, and always gave the crew time to take to their lifeboats. Weddigen was killed in U29 on 18 March 1915 whilst attempting to attack units of the Royal Navy's 4th Battle Squadron. His periscope was seen and U29 was rammed by the battleship HMS Dreadnought. There were no survivors. All Germany mourned.

Emblematic heroes of the Kaiser's new Germany. Weddigen and the crew of U9, depicted on a contemporary propaganda postcard, shortly after each man had been awarded the Iron Cross for sinking the three British cruisers.

With U-boats operating in the North Sea even the Royal Navy's bastion at Scapa Flow in the Orkneys was considered unsafe. The most powerful battle fleet in the world up-anchored and fled to the Lough Swilly in Northern Ireland. In 1916, during the closing stages of the Battle of Jutland, anxiety over imaginary U-boats made Admiral Jellicoe reluctant to pursue aggressively the retreating German battle fleet for fear of being drawn into an ambush of torpedoes and mines. When the lone *U21* sank two British battleships in quick succession during the Gallipoli campaign, pandemonium ensued. In a state of near panic the Admiralty allowed half of the British fleet to withdraw, seriously undermining army operations ashore. These episodes demonstrated for the first – but not the last – time that the presence or fear of a submarine could have a disproportionate impact on a much wider area of operations. In effect, the submarine became a weapon for area denial. This principle could work as well for the British as it did for the Germans. When Max Horton in *E9* sank the light cruiser *Hela* in the German Bight on 12 September 1914, the Germans promptly decided it was far too dangerous to continue using those waters for routine training and exercises and transferred these operations to the Baltic. It did them little good. Horton, Noel Laurence, and later others took their boats through the narrows of the Kattegat and harried the Germans in their own backyard. Although the number of surface warships put out of action was relatively small, the presence of a tiny number of British submarines inhibited German naval activities. More importantly, it also severely disrupted the vital ore traffic from Sweden to Germany's war industries.

Survivors from HMS Hogue, Cressy and Aboukir *after being landed at Harwich. Their serious faces reflect the scale of the disaster in which 1,459 of their shipmates died, a large proportion of them young boys and elderly reservists recalled for wartime duty.*

Roger Keyes, Inspecting Commodore of Submarines, 1910-15. Keyes presided over the 1912 Submarine Development Committee which attempted to define the future operational roles of submarines and produce appropriate designs. To erode Vickers' monopoly on submarine construction, the committee also encouraged other manufacturers to submit designs of their own, none of which proved particularly outstanding. By his own admission, Keyes had a limited understanding of technical matters and even less of logistical planning, as he demonstrated when he sent 'E' boats into the Baltic to support the Russians but omitted to let the Russians know they were coming. Yet as commander of the Harwich flotilla in 1914 and then of the submarines at Gallipoli, he showed Nelsonic leadership qualities, motivating, encouraging and supporting his men, while turning a blind eye to their more outrageous activities.

In support of the Allied landings at Gallipoli, British and French submarines were deployed to the Sea of Marmara to sever Turkish supply lines to the peninsula. The narrow route into the Marmara was extremely hazardous: it was heavily patrolled, stuffed with mines and festooned with anti-submarine nets. Once on station the submarine was isolated and had to fend for itself. Inevitably a number of boats were lost. Others were incredibly successful: Boyle in *E14* and Nasmith in *E11* ran amok through the Turkish sea-lanes. Between May and December 1915, Nasmith alone sank 122 vessels. In the end, the Allied campaign in Gallipoli was a bloody failure, but this was due to the timorousness of senior naval commanders and the incompetence and mendacity of the army high command in France. It was not through any lack of effort, courage or sacrifice on the part of the submariners.

There is nothing new about attacks on merchant ships. They have been happening since humankind first paddled away from the beach, but the motive for piracy has always been individual profit. State-sponsored attacks on maritime trade are a more recent development, with Elizabethan privateers sailing under quasi-legal 'letters of marque'. The concept of close blockade of an enemy's coastline had been applied by the British first during the Napoleonic wars, then again by them against Germany in 1914. The strategic theory of a systematic assault on maritime trade, *'la guerre de course'*, was first formulated by the French in the late 1870s, and they probably had 'perfidious Albion' in mind when they thought of it. Germany was the first to put theory into practice. As the Schlieffen Plan ground to a halt in France, Belgium and Russia, stalled on trench systems, entangled in barbed wire and bogged down in mud, a mass offensive against Britain and Frances' arterial shipping lanes seemed the most expedient method of breaking the stalemate. An all-out U-boat war on trade, *'Handelskreig'* as the Germans called it, had the potential to strangle Britain into submission; it very nearly succeeded.

Under international law attacks on merchant ships were governed by 'Prize Regulations'. These dictated that merchant ships had first to be stopped and searched for contraband; they could not be sunk without warning. Only if the cargo was destined for an enemy port could the ship be sunk and even then only after the crew had manned their lifeboats, had with them adequate supplies of food and water, and been given a course to steer for the nearest shore. It was all very civilized and to their credit most, though not all, U-boat captains adhered to the rules. Obviously the rules of engagement did not apply to attacks on hostile warships, but there were areas of ambiguity in the regulations which opened the way for tragedy. Passenger liners could easily be misidentified, either by accident or deliberately, as armed merchant cruisers and sunk without warning, as could any steamer that carried a gun on deck. Being equipped with a gun, no matter how antiquated and ineffectual, that could theoretically threaten a submarine simply encouraged U-boats to shoot first and ask questions later. But there was no excuse for firing at clearly marked hospital or refugee ships. Such incidents outraged public opinion in neutral countries. When the Cunard liner *Lusitania* was torpedoed in May 1915 killing 1,198 men, women and children, including 128 Americans, the scorn of the world fell upon Germany. More than anything else, fear of antagonizing neutral America and precipitating its entry into the war forced the German government to restrain their U-boats.

V3 at Barrow in 1915. The four boats of the 'V' class were Vickers' response to the 1912 Submarine Committee's request for a new design of coastal submarine, but they had a disappointing performance and were relegated to training duties. V3 was scrapped in 1920.

By the beginning of 1917, Germany's situation was becoming so desperate that it was prepared to risk America's wrath at unrestricted U-boat warfare in the hope that Britain would be forced to sue for peace before America declared war. The onslaught began in February 1917. Germany declared the Atlantic, to a distance of 400 miles from the West Coast of Ireland, a total war zone. The Mediterranean became a blood bath as U-boats hit the heavy traffic coming out of the Suez Canal. In April, 810 merchant ships were sunk, totaling some 860,334 tons. Two months later, 690,000 tons went down with the loss of only two U-boats, and Britain's situation was becoming increasingly precarious. A few perceptive minds at the Admiralty recognised this but could not agree on the solution. British politicians, not the brightest crayons in the box at the best of times, had their eyes fixed on Flanders, mesmerized by Field-Marshal Haig's rhetoric that total victory could only be achieved by further sacrifices on the battlefields of the Western Front.

The problem facing Britain and its Allies was starkly simple: how best to defeat the U-boats. The solution also proved simple, but it took a while to find. From 1915, well-meaning, patriotic citizens had been encouraged to submit ideas for defeating Germany's new weapons to the Board of Invention and Research. Tame cormorants dropping bombs on Zeppelins and trained seagulls searching for periscopes were suggested in all seriousness and were, no doubt, given equally serious and lengthy consideration by the civil servants. Using sea lions to search for submarines was yet another proposal, and the Royal Navy expended considerable effort, and fish, in a feasibility study. Quite how the sea lion was supposed to inform its handler that it had found a U-boat was not explained. Other ideas included using giant magnets, and dumping green paint onto the water to fog periscopes. One suggestion was to be taken seriously: the use of active sound waves to locate and track an underwater target. However, the research and development work that led to sonar would not bear fruit until after the war.

One of a series of British propaganda postcards published by Bamforth & Co during the First World War, always featuring a verse of patriotic sentiment, but rarely showing a submarine. Shown here is A13, last of the 'A' class and the first British submarine to be fitted, albeit experimentally, with a diesel engine.

Initially the Allies put their trust in conventional methods of defense. At great expense, enormous minefields were laid and steel net barrages put into operation, but the U-boats got through both by running on the surface. Q-ships, heavily armed decoys masquerading as innocent merchant ships, were employed in large numbers but the small number of U-boats they destroyed hardly justified the effort. The simple solution, first proposed by the American naval theorist A.T. Mahan back in 1890, was to sail merchant ships in convoys escorted by warships. There was initial resistance to the concept because the Royal Navy much preferred dashing around the oceans with bow waves creaming and battle ensigns flying, to plodding back and forth across the Atlantic shepherding dirty, clapped-out tramp steamers. But as Mahan understood, searching for an elusive raider in the vastness of the ocean was like 'looking for a needle in a haystack'. Convoys brought the enemy into contact. To attack the merchant ships, the U-boats had first to get past the escorts. On the surface the U-boats were too exposed; submerged their slow speed left them outdistanced. Many of the surface warships now had passive hydrophones, less capable than the later sonar, but which could at least alert them to the presence of an underwater attacker. Counter attacks with depth-charges often lacked precision, and an exploding charge had to be almost touching a submarine to destroy it; however, the shock waves and noise from near misses damaged equipment, started leaks and battered the nerves of the U-boat crews. Merchant ships were still being sunk at the end of the war, but they were the ones sailing independently. The implementation of the convoy system lost the U-boats the element of surprise and with it their advantage.

Torpedo compartment of the coastal submarine U21. Surrendered to the Allies in 1918, she was put on public display in Ramsgate harbour. She sank while under tow to the breaker's yard in 1920.

E3 at Barrow in 1912. The 'E' class was similar to the preceding 'D's, but with two significant differences: for the first time watertight bulkheads were installed, and two beam torpedo tubes were fitted for close range attacks. These boats could dive to periscope depth in less than sixty seconds and stay submerged for twenty-four hours. Six of the class were also built as mine layers. Numerically the largest British wartime class, the 'E's bore the brunt of the fighting during the First World War, and men like Horton, Nasmith, Laurence, Boyle and Leir made their reputations in these boats.

On 18 October 1914, E3 achieved the unfortunate distinction of being the first submarine to be sunk by another submarine. Running on the surface in daylight off the Ems estuary, she was hit by a single torpedo from U27 and blew up. Of the fifty-seven boats in the class, nearly half would be lost during the war.

E6 at speed in the Solent.

Norman Holbrook, CO of the elderly and slow B11. On 13 December 1914, Holbrook penetrated the Dardanelles and found the Turkish coastal defence battleship Messudieh at anchor off Chanak. Holbrook sank her with one torpedo. Despite being spun off course by powerful currents, running aground and being fired upon by Turkish artillery, Holbrook successfully extricated B11 and became a public hero. He received the Victoria Cross, the first of five awarded to British submariners in the First World War. The rest of the crew also got medals and all were awarded substantial prize money. It was rather reminiscent of the jubilation that followed Weddigen's action three months earlier and was, perhaps, a reflection of the euphoria that still prevailed in both Britain and Germany before the mass slaughter on the Western Front caused weary resignation to set in.

Kapitanleutnant Otto Hersing, captain of U21. Hersing struck the first blow for the U-boats by sinking HMS Pathfinder on 5 September 1914. In an epic voyage the following year he took his boat through the Mediterranean and Aegean seas to the Dardanelles to attack Allied warships supporting the Gallipoli campaign. On 25 May 1915, Hersing sank the battleship HMS Triumph, diving his boat under his sinking victim to escape the attentions of angry British destroyers. Two days later he struck again and sunk another battleship, HMS Majestic. During the course of the war he sank a total of thirty-six ships and like Weddigen, but unlike several of his colleagues, he scrupulously observed the rules of engagement when attacking merchant ships. Hersing and his crew survived the war; U21 did not. After Germany's surrender, Hersing scuttled his boat as she was being towed into captivity.

Hit by a single torpedo from Hersing's U21, the battleship HMS Majestic sinks off Cape Helles on 27 May 1915. The sinkings of Majestic, and HMS Triumph two days before, had a profoundly demoralizing effect on the Allied troops ashore fighting desperately to maintain a foothold on the Gallipoli peninsula.

AE2 leaving Portsmouth, the second of the two 'E' class boats supplied to the Royal Australian Navy in 1913. AE2 was the first Allied submarine to break into the Turkish Sea of Marmara. She was scuttled by her crew on 30 April 1915 after being heavily damaged by the Turkish destroyer Sultan Hissar. AE1 disappeared off the Bismarck Archipelago in September 1914.

The steam-powered Swordfish on trials in 1916. She was another product of the 1912 Submarine Committee, who wanted a long-range submarine with a surface speed of twenty knots. Such speeds could only be achieved by using steam turbines, an idea that was repeated in the later 'K' class with dreadful consequences. Although Swordfish never saw operational service, she possessed a number of safety features that could, and should, have been fitted to her contemporaries.

E5 as completed. On 28 August 1914, E5 took part in the Heligoland Bight battle, a combined raid of warships and submarines into German waters. Although considered a British victory, it clearly demonstrated the almost impossible task of coordinating submarines with surface units in a wide ranging fleet action. Submarines were better off hunting alone. E5 spent the rest of her life in tedious but vital blockading patrols in the North Sea. She was lost in March 1916. The cause remains unknown.

C31 and C32 in a West Country harbour, with some of their crews on deck having a quiet smoke. Smoking was strictly forbidden inside the early boats due to the ever-present danger of explosive vapours from the petrol engines and hydrogen gas from the lead-acid batteries. The shape of these later 'C' boats has changed radically from the first boats of the class, with the deck casing extended to the bows and the hydroplanes raised higher. Fenders have been rigged to protect the hydroplanes from impact damage.

In January 1915, C31 disappeared without trace whilst conducting a reconnaissance patrol in the approaches to the German occupied port of Zeebrugge. Under the command of Christopher Satow, C32 went to the Baltic in 1916 to help the Russians. On 22 October 1917, with the compass out of action, she ran aground in Vaist Bay, Estonia, and was blown up to prevent the boat's capture by the Germans. A somewhat precipitous action, it later turned out, as the area was still under Russian control.

Navigation was not the strong point of early submariners. What with unreliable compasses, the presence of the enemy, and overcast skies preventing sun or star sights being taken to fix their positions, submariners regularly navigated by dead reckoning, or as one put it, 'by guess and by God'. Not knowing where one was could have fatal consequences, particularly in the North Sea and German Bight, where minefields were all over the place. This may account for C31's disappearance.

Hersing's success in the Mediterranean encouraged Germany to send more U-boats to support its Austrian and Turkish allies. This is U33 in the Marmara, November 1916, heading back to its base at Cattaro on the Adriatic after operations in the Black Sea against the Russians. U33 was commanded by Gansser, who had little time for the niceties of Prize Regulations. As an example of his ruthlessness, in March 1916 he sank the hospital ship Portugal, killing ninety including fifteen nurses.

J4 in 1919 after transfer to the Royal Australian Navy. The 'J' class was yet another attempt at developing a twenty knot submarine that could operate alongside the surface battle fleet and, although seventeen knots was the best they could manage, they were powerful boats with four bow torpedo tubes. Despite their apparent qualities, the Royal Navy wasted little time in getting rid of them after hostilities ended.

CAPTURED GERMAN TORPEDO FROM SUBMARINE. Nº10, COPYRIGHT,

Perfected by the inventor Robert Whitehead, the torpedo was a new weapon in an age of new weapons. Not necessarily better, it was certainly no worse than flame throwers, barbed wire or poison gas. This is a captured Schwartzkopf on display in London during the Great War. German submariners called them 'eels', while the British called theirs 'mouldies', 'tinfish' or just 'fish'. Traditionalists referred to them as the 'Devils device'. Torpedoes, whatever their nationality, were technically complex and difficult to use. A merchant ship steaming slowly in a straight line was an easy and predictable target. A warship at speed and zigzagging evasively was a different kettle of fish altogether, ideally requiring a salvo of four torpedoes fired in a spread to achieve a hit. Most of the early classes had only two bow tubes and, while a full salvo might increase the probability of a hit, it did not guarantee it. An alert target might spot the periscope or the ' feather' of its wake, or see the torpedo tracks or their discharge splash in time to take avoiding action. Launching torpedoes put a submarine seriously out of trim and if tanks were not flooded quickly enough to compensate for the sudden loss of weight and increase in buoyancy the boat could break surface. In these situations, crewmen acting as human ballast sometimes ran from one end of the boat to the other to maintain the trim.

The ideal firing range was about 1,200 yards with a running speed of thirty-five knots, but the torpedo could be fickle in its performance and war-shots often ran too deep. On British boats this was due to a too high discharge pressure in the tubes, with German eels because of problems with the hydrostatic valves that set the running depth. The detonating pistol on British fish also occasionally failed. Given that captains of the early boats fired by eye alone, squinting through the periscope without the benefit of fire-control instruments to compute a 'firing solution', it is a measure of their skill – and luck – that they managed to hit anything at all. Many never did.

45

A merchantman is hit by a U-boat of the Flanders Flotilla out from Zeebrugge. Though dramatic, these four images give only a partial insight into the reality of submarine warfare against maritime trade. Surfaced U-boats and the absence of survivors struggling in the water suggest either that these photos were taken before the implementation of unrestricted sink-without-warning tactics, or that these U-boat captains still held to their traditional naval values and were not prepared to kill defenceless merchant seamen. The carnage of the 1917 'Handelskrieg' looked very different. By 1918, half of all U-boat attacks were carried out at night.

Another victim goes down. The lack of visible damage to the ship's hull and superstructure suggest she has been sunk by the simple expedient of a boarding party opening the sea-cocks or setting scuttling charges.

Sailing vessels were difficult targets to sink. Not valuable enough to waste a torpedo on and, being made of wood, they took a long time to sink no matter how many shells the gun crew pumped into the hull. Burning them was the simplest method, but a column of smoke was likely to bring any warship in the vicinity charging in to investigate.

A calm sea, no debris, no fire, no panic. The crew have been given time to man lifeboats and pull clear before the destruction of their ship – this is almost a scene of tranquility. From a contemporary German perspective these were undoubtedly effective propaganda images, a useful reply to Allied claims that the U-boats were manned by bloodthirsty murderers. Whether these photographs can be regarded as typifying U-boat warfare is debatable. The sinking of the Luisitania was nowhere near so placid.

The hidden for'd gun of the Q-ship HMS Hyderabad. She was specially built for the job, but most Q-ships were converted merchantmen, although trawlers, drifters, yachts, stores carriers and sloops were also used as armed decoys. At the time they were popularly referred to as 'mystery ships' which gave them a romantic, swashbuckling aura but despite all the effort they only managed to sink fourteen U-boats.

Hyderabad's for'd gun unmasked for action. The use of armed decoys may have done more harm than good. Once the U-boats got wise to the danger they became inclined to treat every steamer as a potential Q-ship and, rather than risk surfacing to obey Prize Regulations, use a torpedo instead and sink the ship without warning.

Early in the war C29 was one of several 'C' class boats employed in a distinctly risky method of hunting U-boats. The 'C's were towed submerged by trawlers acting as decoy targets intended to lure unsuspecting Germans into torpedo range of the British submarines. The trick had previously worked twice with other submarine-trawler pairings but, on 29 August 1915, C29 blew up after its towing trawler got lost and wandered into a British minefield.

Captured after getting stranded on a mudbank off Harwich on 27 April 1916, the coastal minelayer UC5 is here being put on public display alongside the Thames Embankment. Mine-laying was an important aspect of submarine operations; although the shallow waters where the lays were often conducted and the explosive cargo made it difficult and dangerous work, it was highly effective, particularly in natural choke points like narrow seaways or harbour approaches.

IMMERSIONE DEL SOTTOMARINO OTARIA   EDIZ FOLCI-SPEZIA

34

Otaria, an Italian 'Glauco' class boat diving at La Spezia. Due to their volatile petrol engines the four 'Glaucos' were relegated to harbour defence duties at Venice and Brindisi during the war. Prior to Italy's declaration of war in 1915, shortages of raw materials had forced the Italian Navy to concentrate on building small craft. The result was a large war time force of sixty-three submarines, but their light construction meant they suffered badly in Adriatic storms and never achieved their full potential.

Artemis, an 'Amphitrite' class boat of the French Navy, spent the war in the Eastern Mediterranean, where French submariners showed both skill and courage stalking U-boats and Austrian shipping in the dangerous waters of the Adriatic. The effectiveness of the French boats was constantly undermined by unreliable diesels and their persistence in using the Drzewiecke torpedo system.

Crewmen of H12 pose for the camera during their boat's transatlantic crossing in 1917. The 'H' class was an American design built by the Bethlehem Steel Company. The first ten came over in 1915, but subsequent boats fell foul of American neutrality laws and were not released until the United States entered the war in 1917.

H44, a British-built version of the original American design. The design was constructed around a single pressure hull and these boats suffered from a lack of reserve buoyancy in consequence. However they could dive in thirty seconds, were very nimble once submerged, and carried a bow salvo of four torpedoes. Several of the class remained in service with the Royal Navy into the Second World War, H44 finally being scrapped in 1944.

An unidentified 'E' boat with the ratings posing exuberantly and the sub-lieutenant on the casing looking self-conscious.

K6 fitted with a raised bow to improve sea-keeping passing a 'Queen Elizabeth' class battleship. The steam-powered 'K' class was the legacy of the Navy's obsession with having a submarine capable of keeping station with the Battle Fleet to protect it from U-boats. The class had an evil reputation, and the only harm they ever inflicted was upon their own crews: five of the class were sunk in accidents, and several others had narrow escapes.

K2 at Rosyth, shortly after the war, with the aft funnel folded back in its diving position. Both funnels, and their attendant hatches and vents, had to be closed down before diving, though the smallest obstruction could jam an opening with dire consequences. Getting a 'K' under could take up to five minutes, ridiculously long when their intended targets could dive in thirty to forty-five seconds.

The beam torpedo compartment of K8 illustrates the size of these boats. Some 330 feet long, very unstable and difficult to keep under control, if dived too steeply the bows could be at crush depth while the stern was still near the surface. The boats also had the disconcerting habit of occasionally refusing to surface for no apparent reason.

The 'L' class was the final major class of the First World War British submarines and evolved directly from the successful 'E's. With a surface range of 3,800 nautical miles, four bow and two beam torpedo tubes, they were an excellent design. This is L1 aground on a Cornish beach while being towed to the breakers yard in March 1930.

L4, launched in November 1917, surfacing after basin trials. Some thirty-four 'L' class boats were completed while a further twenty-five on order were cancelled when hostilities ceased.

E2 in the Mediterranean in 1918 with the crew at diving stations. Sitting at the hydroplane control wheel in the foreground is the boat's Cox'n, PO G. Goodson and behind him sits the 2nd Cox'n, Leading Seamen Eustace. This is a posed photo as the crew are in full uniform and the diving gauge reads 'off'.

The control room of E2 again, this time with the crew in more typical attire. The thick vertical tube is the periscope in the down position and from the relaxed attitudes of the crew the boat is possibly 'bottomed', on the seabed resting the batteries. Behind the PO on the right is the tea urn, some would say the most essential piece of equipment on board.

O1, an 'O' class boat of the US Navy, underway in the Thames River, Connecticut. With a diving depth of 200 feet, 4 bow tubes and a 3in deck gun, the 'O's were useful boats, but they arrived too late to see action. With enormous industrial capacity, America's entry into the war guaranteed Germany's eventual defeat and though the US Navy's surface warships made an important contribution, particularly as convoy escorts, their submarines had no opportunities.

Off Harwich, on 6 July 1918, C25 was caught on the surface and strafed by German floatplanes, killing the boat's CO, three lookouts on the bridge and two men in the conning tower. With a body jamming the conning tower hatch and her hull perforated by bullets, C25 was unable to dive and lay crippled and helpless until rescued by the destroyer HMS Lurcher. This incident was a hint of things to come in the Second World War, when the aeroplane would become the greatest threat to a submarine's survival.

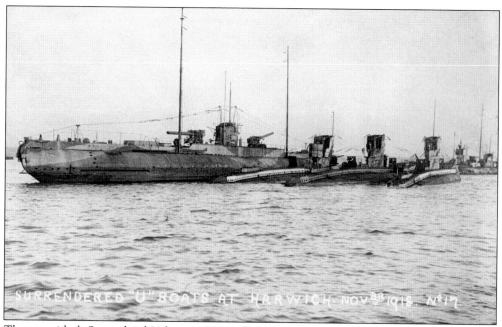

The vanquished. Surrendered U-boats at Harwich in November 1918.

The victors on the vanquished. Lt Blackburn and the prize crew who brought the surrendered cruiser U-boat U155 into London's St Catherines Dock for public display.

OSTENDE -SOUS-MARIN ALLEMAND-
-GERMAN SUBMARIN-

A U-boat at Ostende destroyed by its own crew before the retreat from Belgium. Although the German army remained largely undefeated on the Western Front, civilian morale had collapsed under the privations resulting from the Royal Navy's blockade, and red flags of revolution and mutiny fluttered from the mastheads of the Imperial German Navy's battleships. But the U-boat men, theoretically beaten, came home with their morale intact and battle ensigns flying. By the end, Germany had lost 178 U-boats and over 4,000 men. The Royal Navy lost 56 submarines and 1,174 men. This was hardly a large number compared to the vast slaughter on land, but was still a significantly high proportion of both navies' submarine forces. Not that such statistics were much consolation to the relatives of the submariners who never came home.

Three

Between the Wars

After the 'war to end all wars' had ended, the British promptly chose to ignore any lessons that might have been learnt, with the Admiralty preferring to pretend the U-boat campaign had never happened. No staff analysis of the strategic campaign was conducted, nor was any assessment made of U-boat battle tactics. This astonishing lapse would later have serious repercussions. Instead, the British expended considerable effort in trying to get submarines banned outright at successive international naval conferences and, when this failed, put their faith in ASDIC as their panacea protection against the underwater menace. The Royal Navy persisted, against all the evidence and hard-won experience, in attempting to integrate their own submarines with the surface fleet. Dozens of submariners paid for this misguided policy with their lives.

Men of the 12th Submarine Flotilla at their St Valentine's Day dance, 1919. Usually organized by the flotilla captain's wife, only respectable young ladies would be invited to such functions. Ladies of, say, a less respectable disposition had to be met in the pubs and hotels outside the dockyard gates.

To be fair, everyone else also had rather blinkered views. The United States recognized the value of the submarine, and in the 1930s put into production a series of superb long-range boats capable of extended operation far into the Pacific, where Japan was now perceived as the major potential threat to American interests. Yet in their strategic planning they overlooked the fundamental geo-economic fact that Japan, an island nation whose heavy industries were dependant on imported raw materials, was as vulnerable to 'guerre de course' as Britain. In a possible future war, priority targets for US submarines were to be the heavy surface units of the Japanese navy, not the vulnerable and vital merchantmen. Also, the advantages gained from their submarines' superior design features were largely negated by grossly unrealistic training exercises, which tended to instill attitudes of extreme caution in the commanders. The Americans further failed to appreciate the value of the convoy system, and their own merchant ships would later suffer badly as a result.

Japan, Britain's former ally in the Far East, had begun its slide into expansionist militarism, accelerated by insensitive American attitudes and patronizing racism from the other major powers in the League of Nations. Such factors convinced the Japanese Army that the only way to expand their nation's 'sphere of economic influence' and guarantee supplies of essential raw materials was through military conquest. The Japanese Navy, being more cerebral, was less convinced, but deference to the côterie around the Emperor overcame caution. The key to Japanese military expansion lay in the removal of American naval power from the Pacific region. Despite the audacity and tactical brilliance of the future Pearl Harbour strike, the Japanese plan was rigid and hierarchical, rather like a game of chess. As in chess, no deviation from the rules was permitted. Submarines were only to attack the valuable battleships, aircraft carriers and heavy cruisers of the US Pacific Fleet: anything else was irrelevant. So the plan, coupled with the tradition of unwavering obedience to orders and authority, stifled initiative and imagination and handicapped offensive patrol operations.

Between the two wars all major navies regarded heavy naval surface units as the principal targets for their submarines. Surprisingly, given their recent practical demonstration to the contrary, so did the Germans. Under the terms of the Treaty of Versailles, Germany was forbidden to possess submarines but circumvented this ban by establishing a covert research bureau in Holland, where designs were developed for commercial export to Spain, Turkey and Finland. Finland also secretly trained a new generation of German submariners. When Hitler came to power in 1933, U-boat construction began in German yards but remained a relatively low priority within the overall scheme of German rearmament.

In 1935, the man who is forever associated with the concept of rapacious unrestrained submarine warfare was appointed supreme commander of the U-boat service. Karl Dönitz was a career naval officer and enthusiastic Nazi whose knowledge of submarines was limited to two years operational experience in the final years of the Great War. He had, however, considerable organizational ability and a shrewd understanding of tactical doctrine, having spent much time developing operational tactics for massed night attacks. This would later have a devastating impact during the Battle of the Atlantic. Nevertheless, at the time of his appointment, Dönitz regarded the wartime role of the submarine in much the same way as his conservative contemporaries in Britain, America and Japan. By 1938, his opinion had changed and he published a book outlining precisely his strategy for conducting a submarine campaign against maritime trade. Nobody in Britain read it.

For some British submariners the war did not end in 1918. In May 1919, the 7th Flotilla sailed for the Baltic to support Lithuania, Estonia and Latvia's struggle for independence from Bolshevik Russia. The E27 and L11 are seen here at Revel, Estonia, in June 1919.

E9 in the floating dock at Revel. The disk visible on the side of the starboard ballast tank is part of the Fessenden underwater signaling gear. The 7th Flotilla came home in September 1919, but not without loss; L55 had been sunk with all hands by Russian shellfire in June.

H47 *at Campbeltown in March 1919. On 9 July 1929, running on the surface off the Welsh coast, in broad daylight and calm weather, she inexplicably collided with L12.* H47 *sank like a stone, taking all but three of her crew with her.*

'K' boats of the 1st Flotilla visiting Algiers, c.1924. Ominously, K22 was originally numbered K13. On 29 January 1917 she sank when the engine-room flooded during diving trials. After a fraught rescue operation forty-six survivors finally escaped fifty-seven hours later. Re-numbered and a year later, during a night exercise in the Firth of Forth between her flotilla and the Grand Fleet, K22 rammed K14 and was in turn hit by the battlecruiser HMS Inflexible and nearly capsized. In the chaos K4 and K17 were sunk, three boats were seriously damaged, and 103 men killed. With typically grim humour, submariners named it the 'Battle of May Island'.

Some of K5's crew displaying their sports trophies in September 1920. Sitting in the centre is K5's thirty-three year old CO, Lt Cdr John Austin Gaimes, DSO. He had only three months left to live. During exercises 120 miles off the Scilly Isles, K5 dived and disappeared. Only a few pieces of wood and the lid of a sailor's 'ditty' box floating in an oil slick were found.

The officer's wardroom on K8. The comparative luxury of the fittings was due more to the extra space in these large boats than a sudden concern by the Admiralty for the well-being of submariners. But at least the comfort of the wardroom helped soothe the frayed nerves of 'K' boat officers. That, and pink gins.

Boats of the 1st Flotilla, c.1922. Alongside K6 is the new monitor submarine M2.

M1 *at Fortrose, Scotland in 1921. Three 'M' class boats were completed, each fitted with a 12in battleship's gun. Much to everyone's surprise, the enormous gun housing improved stability and buoyancy, but this did not help the 'M's escape the misfortune that cursed their close relatives, the 'K's.*

Surfacing off Start Point on 12 November 1925, M1 *was rammed by the steamer SS* Vidar. *The impact ripped the gun from its mounting, puncturing the pressure hull, and* M1 *sank with all sixty-nine crewmen. A recent survey of the wreck suggests some in the engine-room may have survived the sinking but perished while attempting an escape.*

M2 at Gibraltar in 1931 after conversion to a seaplane carrier. This was a bizarre experiment considering the old buffers at the Admiralty disliked aeroplanes even more than submarines. The tactical advantage gained by increasing the M2's reconnaissance range was outweighed by the boat's vulnerability during the slow process of launching and recovering the aircraft, and cutting corners to reduce this time probably contributed to the boat's loss.

H34 surfacing in Portsmouth harbour. In the background is the cruiser HMS Calypso, with L26 moored in the corner of the basin. Until the arrival of more modern designs, the 'H' and 'L' classes formed the backbone of the inter-war Submarine Service.

With wings folded, the purpose-built Parnall Peto floatplane is visible inside M2's hanger. For obvious reasons, submariners do not much like holes in their boats and the cavernous opening to the hanger must have caused apprehension. Even on calm water the limited freeboard is apparent. M2 foundered off Portland on 26 January 1932, when the hanger flooded. All sixty men on board drowned.

GIBRALTAR. 2.2.22.

The 3rd Flotilla at Gibraltar on 2 February 1922. Seven days later H24 would be involved in a potentially fatal collision. Seven weeks later, H42 would be lost with all hands in virtually identical circumstances.

Close view of Damage sustained

During combined fleet exercises on 9 February, the destroyer HMS Vancouver rammed H24 as she surfaced, slicing open the conning tower. Fortunately, the pressure hull was not ruptured and H24 survived. With her ripped conning tower clearly visible, H24 is taken in tow by the cruiser HMS Curacoa.

S/M. H 52. *Winning Skiffs race 3rd S/m. Flotilla. 18/3/22*
GIBRALTAR

A moment of light relief in a bleak month for the 3rd Flotilla, as crewmen from H52 win the Flotilla's skiff race at Gibraltar on 18 March 1922.

HMS Versatile in Gibraltar's dry dock after the fatal collision with H42 on 23 March. Given this degree of keel damage resulting from an unintentional impact with a submarine, it is easy to see why the Admiralty in the Second World War ordered hard pressed convoy escorts not to ram U-boats.

Wreaths for the twenty-six men who died in H42.

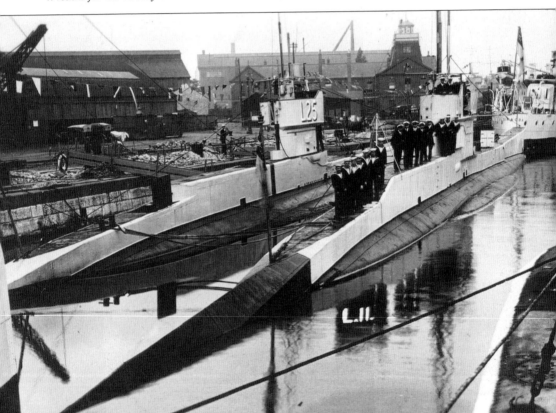

The minelayers L25 and L11 at Chatham with the cruiser HMS Curacoa moored ahead. One of the storage chutes for the 'eggs' is just visible on L25's starboard ballast tank, while those on L11 have been plated over.

L19 on the China Station, with her torpedo recovery derrick rigged on the casing and an improvised awning rigged on the conning tower for shade. The 'L's spent much of their working lives in the Far East, to the delight of their crews who enjoyed the charms of both warm exotic locations and warm exotic ladies.

Three 'L' class boats in dry dock at Hong Kong, their bow tubes clearly visible.

The control room of L23, showing the hydroplane wheels and their depth gauges.

Oberon *launching at Chatham Dockyard on 24 September 1926. She marked the recommencment of British submarine construction, but was not a great success, suffering constant mechanical problems and leakage from the riveted fuel tanks. As a result her crew got far more shore leave than was usual. Hence her unofficial name, 'Oh Be Joyful'.*

L24 on the China Station preparing to recover a practice torpedo, with a swimmer in the water attaching a line to the torpedo derrick. In yet another collision, L24 was lost with all forty-three crew after being rammed by the battleship HMS Resolution off Portland Bill in January 1924.

Fort Blockhouse, Gosport, with the 'trots' full, c.1930. On the far left is Orpheus from the new 'Odin' class, with M2 in the row astern. Visible in the right background are Semaphore Tower, home of Flag Officer Portsmouth, and the masts of HMS Victory.

X1 *at Malta. With her four 5.2in quick-firing guns X1, theoretically, could have engaged a destroyer, although with her lack of armour she would have been foolish to do so.*

X1 *diving in the Mediterranean. X1 had great potential as a commerce raider but old opinions died hard and sinking merchant ships was just not British. She was laid up in 1933 and then scrapped before she gave ideas to anyone else.*

The Italian Balilla returning to La Spezia in 1929 after torpedo trials. A large cruiser submarine intended for commerce raiding in the Red Sea and Indian Ocean as part of Mussolini's grandiose dream of a new Roman Empire, Balilla proved too big for wartime operations in the restricted waters of the Mediterranean and was laid up in April 1941.

Two French 'Ariane' class boats in the basin at Rochefort, c.1930. An unusual feature of this class was a complicated swiveling twin torpedo mount abaft the conning tower, visible here on the right-hand boat trained to starboard.

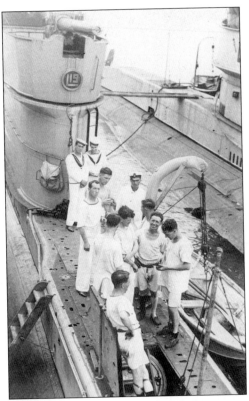

L19 *on the China Station, with some of her crew wearing the scanty working rig necessary in the Far East. Tropical heat made living conditions onboard very unpleasant and in the next war British submariners suffered badly, particularly from 'prickly heat'. This was in marked contrast to US Navy submariners who enjoyed the benefits of air conditioning, showers, and ice cream machines.*

At least submariners finally had the luxury of bunks, but they had to be shared, a practice known as 'hot bunking': as one man went on duty, the bunk would be taken by another coming off watch. The tea 'fanny' takes pride of place on the mess table, reflecting how such small comforts made life a bit more tolerable.

'L' boats in dry dock at Hong Kong, showing the rarely seen propellers, rudders, and aft hydroplanes.

The depot ship HMS Cyclops at Venice with a 'River' class boat on her starboard side, 'O' and 'R' classes to port and Oberon heading for the open sea.

The launch of *Capitan O'Brien* for the Chilean Navy at Vickers-Armstrong's Barrow yard, 2 October 1929. Developed from the Royal Navy's 'O' class, she remained in service until 1957. Vickers was a major supplier of submarines to foreign navies such as Chile, Portugal, and Estonia.

HMS *Oswald* at Fort Blockhouse, with Camper & Nicholson's boatyard in the background. The prominent ram bow was the distinctive feature of the 'O' class. *Oswald* was later sunk in the Mediterranean by the Italian destroyer *Vivaldi*, which rescued the survivors.

Olympus at Chinwangtao on 4 August 1934. Designed as overseas boats to protect British interests in the Far East, the 'O's spent most of their time before the war on the China Station. Olympus later ran supplies to beleaguered Malta, but hit a mine off the island in May 1942. There were twelve survivors.

Having won the Fleet's water polo cup, Olympus' team pose for the camera onboard their depot ship HMS Medway, at Wei-Hai-Wei in 1934.

Pandora *in the Far East. When war came,* Pandora *went to the Mediterranean commanded by 'Tubby' Linton who became one of the most successful British submariners.* Pandora *was bombed in Malta harbour on 1 April 1942. Linton would be killed in* Turbulent, *sunk by depth-charges off Corsica in March 1943. He had destroyed 90,000 tons of shipping and was posthumously awarded the Victoria Cross.*

Regent's *4in gun, with* Rover *alongside. The raised gun mounting was a feature of many British boats of this period, allowing the gun to be brought into action before the boat was fully surfaced, while the high coaming protected the crew in rough seas.* Regent *disappeared in the Adriatic in April 1943, probably mined.* Rover *survived the war and was broken up in 1946.*

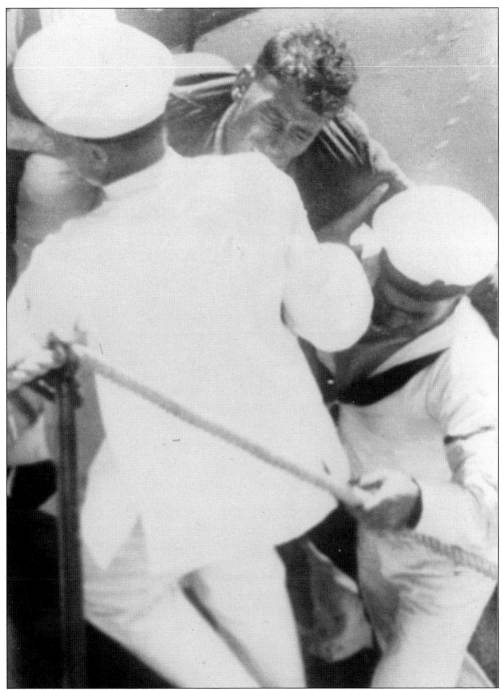

On 9 June 1931, in a misty North China Sea, the Chinese steamer Yuta *accidentally rammed HMS Poseidon, rupturing the pressure hull just forward of the conning tower. There was no panic and thirty-one men escaped before the boat sank in 120 feet of water, but eighteen died in the after ends, and eight were trapped in the bow torpedo compartment. Led by Petty Officer Willis, they finally escaped using the recently issued Davis Submarine Escape Apparatus (DSEA), although only four made it to the surface alive. Here one of the survivors is being helped onboard the aircraft carrier HMS Hermes.*

The depot ship HMS Medway with 'O' and 'P' boats of the 4th Flotilla at Wei-Hai-Wei in 1933. From left to right: Parthian, Olympus, Osiris, and Pandora. Both Parthian and Olympus have their wireless masts rigged, the height being necessary for effective W/T communication in these regions.

L'Espoir and Ajax, 'Redoutable' class boats of the French Navy at Algiers, c.1935. These ocean-going boats were well liked by their crews for their high surface speed and good handling characteristics. After France's surrender, L'Espoir joined the Vichy Navy and was scuttled at Toulon when the Germans occupied Vichy France in November 1942.

Despite the reputation of 'The Trade' for being smelly and dirty, submariners could, when occasion demanded, look as impressive as sailors from the Royal Yacht.

Illern and Bavern of the Swedish Navy. Wisely perceiving both Germany and Russia as potential aggressors, and determined to preserve independence and neutrality, Sweden owned one of the strongest navies in the Baltic with a large submarine force. The investment paid off: although encircled by Germany, Sweden remained free.

SECOND APPEARANCE OF H.M.S. THETIS, MOLFRE BAY

One final tragedy struck the Royal Navy's Submarine Service before the war. On 1 June 1939, the brand-new 'T' class boat HMS Thetis, with 103 men onboard, plunged into the mud in Liverpool Bay on her first dive. Though the stern was above water at low tide, it took some time to locate the wreck and still longer to commence rescue operations. Four men managed to escape before the remainder succumbed to carbon dioxide poisoning. What began as a hopeful rescue became a depressing salvage operation, which took place in full view of newsreel and press photographers. The public was appalled by the disaster; the more so when it became apparent that the accident was a result of two small errors in construction and design which gave misleading information, starting a chain of events culminating in the uncontrollable flooding of the fore ends. It was a stark reminder that the smallest oversight or mistake in a submarine can have disastrous consequences. The salvage operation proved extremely difficult. Finally, at 2:30pm on Monday 23 October, the bows broke surface, nearly four months after the fatal dive.

Poignant and forlorn, the salvaged Thetis lies beached in Moelfre Bay.

A specialist mine rescue team from the Staffordshire coalfields carried out the grim task of removing the ninety-nine bodies.

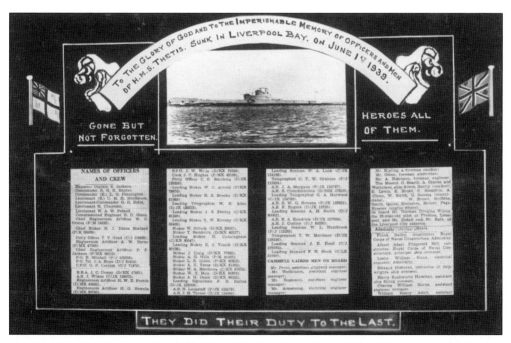

An 'In Memorium' postcard published immediately after the accident. Thetis was subsequently repaired and re-commissioned as HMS Thunderbolt, serving with distinction in the Mediterranean until she was sunk with all hands by the Italian corvette Cicogna in March 1943.

Type IIB coastal U-boats fitting out at the Germania Works at Kiel in 1935.

U12, U17 and U13 at Travemunde. Nicknamed 'Dugout Canoes', the small Type IIs were mostly relegated to training duties from the end of 1939. On their bows are saw-tooth net-cutters, a feature common to early U-boats but later dropped as irrelevant in the light of wartime experience. The wire loop on U12's conning tower is an early radio direction finder.

Four

World War Two

Although the Battle of Britain has become enshrined in popular folklore as saving the country from Nazi invasion, the Battle of the Atlantic was the pivotal campaign. If Hitler had won it, the invasion of Britain would have been quite unnecessary; the country would have been starved and strangled into submission, forced to accept whatever terms Germany dictated. Britain's defeat might not have happened overnight, but it would have happened eventually.

Type IIB U-boats of the 'Weddigen Flotilla', based at Kiel, exercising in the Baltic in 1935.

For Dönitz, Britain's declaration of war on 3 September came as something of a shock. He had been assured by Hitler that war with Britain was unlikely before 1942 at the earliest and the U-boat building programme had been planned accordingly. Only twenty U-boats were on patrol when war broke out, and the distances involved in operating from their home bases in Germany restricted their radius of action to areas around the British Isles. Determined not to repeat past mistakes and antagonise a staunchly neutral American public, the U-boats also operated under the restrictions of Prize Regulations. After the fall of France in 1940 and the capture of the ports of Brest, Lorient, Bordeaux, and St Nazaire, the U-boats were able to strike deep into the mid-Atlantic without having to circumnavigate the heavily patrolled waters around Britain. From this moment merchant shipping losses began to rise steadily. In October 1940, 352,000 tons of shipping were sunk. By April 1941, British, Allied and neutral losses had risen to 687,901 tons. The U-boat crews called it 'the happy time'.

This time at least there was no prevarication over instigating the convoy system, although the Royal Navy was initially more anxious about surface commerce raiders, like *Graf Spee*. That merchant shipping suffered heavy losses was not due to flaws in the convoy system but to inadequate defences and a failure by the British to understand U-boat tactics. There was also a shortage of escort ships. One of the more pernicious myths about the Second World War is that the pre-war climate of pacifism hindered Britain's naval rearmament. This claim is bogus. The Royal Navy had plenty of destroyers, but a large proportion of them were tied down protecting the battleships. True, these destroyers found it heavy going in the short, steep seas of the North Atlantic, but they were better than nothing. The frigates and corvettes that later played such a vital role in defending the convoys evolved directly from hard-won wartime lessons, unforeseeable before the war. The Royal Navy also relied on ASDIC to provide blanket protection. This tactic was not unreasonable if the U-boats were submerged, but their standard massed wolf-pack attacks were carried out on the surface, invariably overwhelming the hard-pressed escorts.

A subtle British propaganda postcard distributed in neutral Portugal early in the war. Aircraft would later play a major role in defeating the U-boats.

Swordfish, lead boat of the 'S' class. Some sixty-two were built, making it the largest British class. Swordfish vanished without trace off Ushant in November 1940.

The escort's task was made more difficult by the U-boat's ability to manoeuvre better, go faster and dive much deeper than the Allies initially realised; the Type VIIC could descend to 660 feet. ASDIC contact on the target was lost as the hunting ship closed in on the U-boat and exploding depth-charges disrupted the transmissions. Experienced U-boat COs could judge the moment to make a sharp course alteration to evade falling charges by listening to the ASDIC 'pings' bouncing off their boat.

Although not apparent at the time, the tide began to turn slowly against the U-boats in 1941 as the escorts began to employ a coordinated convoy defence. In March, Dönitz lost Prien, Kretschmer and Schepke, his top three aces. The effect on the German public and the U-boat arm was traumatic, but the battle continued to rage across the Atlantic. When the USA entered the war in December, Dönitz deployed boats to the American seaboard and Caribbean where they had a second 'happy time' amongst the unescorted merchant ships sailing independently. November 1942 and March 1943 saw the worst losses of the war, with 693,000 tons of shipping going down in March alone. Losses of merchant ships had begun to exceed their rate of replacement, and amongst senior Allied commanders the fear was growing that convoys on the North Atlantic route would have to be suspended. However, the unlimited industrial resources of the USA and the introduction of new weapons were beginning to have an affect.

The Second World War was a war of technology. Not the crude technology of the 1914-19 war, but a race between scientists to develop sophisticated systems that could locate, decode or jam the opposing systems of the enemy. These systems were, however, mounted on conventional vehicles which, though bigger, faster and more complex, were in essence not that dissimilar to their predecessors. And human beings still had to operate them. Nowhere was the impact of the new technology more significant than in the war at sea, and in the Battle of the Atlantic it was decisive.

The key technology was electronics in the form of radar, radio, and signals intelligence. In June 1942, ASV (air-to-surface-vessel) radar was introduced on the maritime patrol aircraft of RAF Coastal Command, while by July most Royal Navy escorts were fitted with Type 271 centimetric radar capable of detecting a U-boat's conning tower at ranges up to 5,000 yards. By December, the escorts were also using high frequency radio direction finding (HF/DF), colloquially known as 'Huff-Duff'. To some extent all submarine commands over-controlled their boats at sea, but Dönitz was worse than most, incessantly bombarding his boats with signals demanding acknowledgements and information. Using HF/DF, the escorts were now able to home onto U-boat radio transmissions, while convoys could be routed away from known concentrations of U-boats. Finally, but no less importantly, the cipher experts at Bletchley Park, using captured Enigma machines and Alan Turing's analogue computer, had broken the Kriegsmarines codes.

The key factor tipping the scales against the U-boats was the aeroplane. In October 1942, the four-engined Halifax, with a payload of six 600lb depth bombs armed with Torpex explosive, entered service with Coastal Command, who commenced an all-out offensive over the Bay of Biscay. Until then the Bay had been a private lake for the U-boats. Outward bound from their French bases, or returning from patrol, the U-boats were accustomed to an undisturbed surface passage. Using ASV radar, high intensity flares or the simple 'moonpath' method, aircraft thundered out of the Biscay night raking decks and conning towers with gunfire, and with depth-charges dropping from bomb bays. Karl Wahnig, formerly of U802, said submariners came to fear air attack more than any other threat. With beefed-up flak guns, the U-boats often stayed on the surface to fight back but losses continued to rise. Much of this effort would have been unnecessary if RAF Bomber Command had attacked the fortified U-boat pens in France while they were under construction, but this was regarded as a 'defensive' tactic and was not to be countenanced. The German construction yards were bombed instead – this being 'offensive' action – to no effect. In April 1943 the introduction of very long range B24 Liberators closed the mid-Atlantic air-gap, while the introduction of the mass-produced 'Woolworth' escort carriers operating with specialised hunter-killer escort groups finally provided a total aerial blanket over the convoys. In May 1943, thirty-one U-boats were sunk in twenty-three days and Dönitz was forced to withdraw his boats from the North Atlantic. Although merchant ships continued to be sunk, the wolf-packs would never again have the easy pickings of 'the happy time'.

Along with the new weapons came new anti-submarine warfare (ASW) tactics. Dedicated, experienced escort groups led by men like Capt Macintyre and Cdr Walker, employing rehearsed manoeuvres exotically named 'Buttercup', 'Raspberry' and 'Pineapple', using the 'creeping attack' to pin down a U-boat with ASDIC while another escort moved in to drop a depth-charge pattern, contributed to the defeat of the U-boats. But some attitudes remained slow to change. 'Guns', said a British officer inspecting a newly arrived Canadian corvette, 'guns will win this war'. He was, consequently, not best pleased on opening an ammunition locker to find it stuffed full with bottles of smuggled whisky.

Seahorse *and the large minelayer* Narwhal *alongside the depot ship HMS Lucia. Both submarines were early casualties.* Seahorse *was depth-charged in the Heligoland Bight on 7 January 1940.* Narwhal, *after successful lays in the Skagerrak and Kattegat, was lost in July.*

In this war of attrition, the material superiority of the Allies proved overwhelming. It also contributed to the physical exhaustion, shattered nerves and faltering morale of the U-boat crews, while their skills became diluted through the loss of their most experienced men and their replacement by inadequately trained recruits and party apparatchiks. Yet given the destruction wrought by German submarines, it is a sobering thought that of approximately 870 U-boats sent into action, 550 never sank anything at all.

The Battle of the Atlantic demonstrated the power of the submarine but also its vulnerability when confronted by determined and capable ASW forces. The Royal Navy's submarines were up against such forces right from the start, having no option but to engage the enemy on his own doorstep, in waters that were often shallow, always heavily mined and vigorously patrolled, both by aircraft and ships. Despite inevitable heavy casualties, the persistence, courage and tenacity of British submariners produced some telling results.

The German conquest of Norway tends to be perceived as a swift and easy victory. What is often overlooked is the heavy damage suffered by the *Kriegsmarine* during the campaign, much of it inflicted by British submarines. The cruisers *Karlsruhe* and *Bremse* were sunk outright, the pocket battleship *Lutzow* had her stern virtually blown off by a salvo from *Spearfish*, and *Clyde* put a single torpedo into the battle-cruiser *Gneisnau*, putting her out of action for six months. At least eleven large transports, three tankers, six minesweepers, a U-boat and several miscellaneous vessels also went down from the torpedoes and mines of the British boats. As a result, for the rest of the war, nothing moved along the Norwegian coast without a heavy escort.

It was in the Mediterranean theatre that British submarines really made their presence felt. The massive aerial bombardment inflicted upon Malta was largely due to the presence there of the 10th Submarine Flotilla, whose boats were a permanent thorn in the Axis supply lines. British losses were very heavy. The clear waters of the Mediterranean and Aegean were dangerous places for submarine operations; of eighteen British boats sunk in 1942, fifteen went down in the Mediterranean. Despite the conditions, most of the British aces, such as Wanklyn, Linton, Miers, and Bryant, achieved their successes in these waters, interdicting the sea lanes carrying the supplies essential to the Italian and German armies in North Africa. Tankers were priority targets and their destruction seriously undermined Rommel's ability to fight. In October 1942, 44 per cent of all fuel sent was destroyed in transit. Submarines may well also be considered the single most important factor in defeating the Axis campaign in North Africa.

For British submarines arriving in the Pacific it was largely a case of too little, too late. Though some notable and spectacular successes were had, most of the damage had already been done by the US Navy, whose submarines had sunk just about every ship in the Japanese merchant fleet. It was a classic demonstration of '*guerre de course*' and Japan paid a heavy price.

The 'Bull of Scapa Flow', Gunther Prien, CO of U47. On the night of 13/14 October 1939, Prien penetrated the incomplete defences of the Royal Navy's base at Scapa Flow and put a salvo into the battleship Royal Oak. A magazine blew up, and she rolled over and sank with the loss of 833 men. U47 returned home to wild adulation. Prien was awarded the Knight's Cross by Hitler personally, and the rest of the crew each received the Iron Cross. It was a major propaganda coup, made better by Prien being an ardent supporter of the Nazi Party.

U47, Prien's personal emblem painted on the conning tower, returns in triumph to Kiel. Behind, the crew of the Emden cheer the boat in. Out in the Atlantic, Prien would become one of the leading U-boat aces until his death in March 1941. In a running convoy battle lasting five hours, U47 was heavily depth-charged and plunged out of control. An explosion lit the depths, one witness even seeing flames briefly dancing on the surface. It was an apocalyptic end of appropriately Wagnerian proportions.

O23 at Rotterdam shortly after its launch in December 1939. Armed with four bow, two midships and two stern tubes, four anti-aircraft guns, with a high surface speed and capable of diving to 320 feet, she was a powerful boat. When the Wehrmacht overran Holland in May 1940, O23 escaped to England and joined the Dutch Navy in exile. She fought initially in the Mediterranean before sailing to the Far East where she conducted several 'cloak and dagger' operations. She was scrapped in 1949.

Snapper *departing Malta in 1937. Under her CO, William King,* Snapper *did much damage to enemy supply convoys during the German invasion of Norway in April 1940. King served continuously in submarines throughout the war and afterwards became a solo yachtsman, in reaction to his wartime experiences.* Snapper *and her crew disappeared without trace in the Bay of Biscay in February 1941.*

Seawolf, *another 'S' boat that fought in the Norwegian campaign, sank the 6,000 ton* Hamm *off the Skaw in a night attack. The clear water and long hours of light from the Arctic's midnight sun made these waters a dangerous place for submarines.* Seawolf *survived. Several others did not.*

On the evening of 9 April 1940, the cruiser Karlsruhe was torpedoed and sunk by Truant. In return, Truant suffered a heavy and prolonged counter-attack from the escorts. With machinery damaged, air and batteries virtually exhausted, Truant finally surfaced and limped home to a hero's welcome.

The wolf-packs gather. Type VIIA U-boats at Wilhelmshaven. From left to right: U34, U28, U29, U30 and U36.

A Type VIIC in the Atlantic. This boat is only a few days into its patrol as the lookout is still clean-shaven. Fresh water was far too precious to waste on shaving. The two flanges encircling the middle and top of the conning tower are spray and wind deflectors, with the short post on the fore casing the underwater sound detection apparatus. There were more Type VIIC submarines built than any other, and they formed the backbone of the U-boat arm.

A Type VIIC coming alongside a supply ship. Replenishing U-boats at sea was a constant headache. Initially, German-American oil magnates sent tankers out into the Atlantic to refuel the boats but this ceased when the US entered the war. Surface supply ships were too vulnerable anyway. Type XIV supply submarines were used instead, rendezvousing with their customers in remote places with fresh ammunition, fuel, and water. Cumbersome and unwieldy, these 'milch cows' were systematically hunted down and sunk by the Allies.

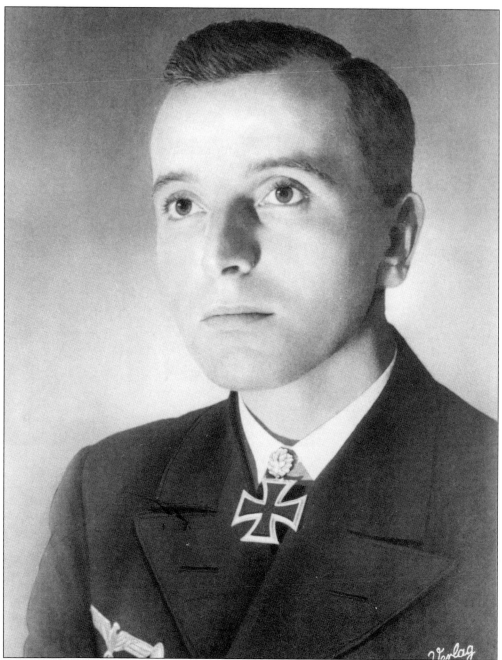

Otto Kretschmer – with 314,000 tons sunk, the highest scoring submariner of the Second World War. A dedicated professional naval officer, 'Silent Otto' was the total opposite of the ostentatious Prien. Like all successful submarine captains, Kretschmer meticulously planned for every eventuality and rigorously trained his crew accordingly. His technique was to attack on the surface at night, relying on the high speed and small silhouette of his boat to dodge the escort screen and penetrate the convoy. This worked while the escorts were few and the defences disorganized. It ceased to work when they grew more proficient. On 17 March 1941 his boat was sunk and Kretschmer and most of his crew captured. Post-war, Kretschmer served in the reconstituted Bundesmarine, rising to the rank of Admiral.

Loading 'eels' on a Type VII. The dome at the base of the conning tower houses the magnetic compass. In the early stages of the war, Germany, America and Britain had problems with their torpedoes, particularly with the exploders which occasionally detonated prematurely or failed to go bang at all. Royal Navy sailors on surface ships generally dismissed torpedoes as 'the main ornament'. Despite the initial difficulties, both German and American submariners had the advantage of being able to programme a target's bearing into their torpedoes before firing, removing the necessity for the boat to be pointing directly at the target. British boats, firing a spread salvo, had to do so 'on the swing'. They were, however, firing the 21in MK VIII ** torpedo. With a range of 7,500 yards running at forty knots, driven by a four cylinder semi-diesel, and with an 805lb Torpex warhead, it was devastating, providing it hit. Introduced in 1927, MK VIII's remained in Royal Navy service until 1989. By late 1943, Germany had introduced both FAT, an anti-convoy torpedo that zigzagged until it found a target, and the T5 Zaunkonig acoustic homing torpedo, which was not very successful. Kretchmer believed in making every shot count; aiming carefully and only firing one torpedo at each target, but he was exceptional and operating when the U-boats held the tactical advantage. Despite the technological advances, some things had not changed since the last war. Clear thinking and a good eye were essential, and a torpedo attack remained difficult and fraught with danger.

A munitions ship goes up. Rarely did anyone survive such a cataclysm.

Survivors from a torpedoed merchantman being rescued. These were the lucky ones. Merchant seamen are the forgotten victims of submarine warfare: one in four was killed during the Battle of the Atlantic. Overall 33,000 British seamen lost their lives.

The principal anti-submarine weapon has always been the depth-charge, either rolled off the stern or, as here, mounted on a thrower to spread the pattern. With a hydrostatic pistol set to explode the charge at a pre-determined depth, effectiveness was dependent on an accurate estimation of the target's depth.

An 'ash-can' on shallow setting exploding. Impressive from the surface, this was nerve-wracking underneath. Yet the sea is a submarine's best protection. Thermal and density variations distort active sonar transmissions, though passive hydrophones might still pick up the soft 'weep weep' of a boat's propellers or their cavitation if revolving too fast at shallow depth. To be safe: go deep and keep quiet.

The Russian Kumzha from the 'Red-banner' Baltic Fleet. Depicted in the vignette is her CO, III Rank Captain F.G. Vershinin, posthumously awarded the title 'Hero of the Soviet Union' after the Kumzha was sunk off Porkkala by Finnish sub-chasers on 15 October 1942.

A member of the 'SHCH' Series V class, Kumzha was a medium submarine armed with four bow and two stern torpedo tubes, with a range of 5,750 nautical miles, and an operating depth of 300 feet. By the time of the German invasion in June 1941, the Soviet Union had a large force of 210 submarines in service. However, despite the courage and gallantry of their crews, their effectiveness was undermined by inadequate training, a shortage of capable officers after Stalin's purges, and an inflexible bureaucratic command structure that supplied plenty of political dogma but little useful naval intelligence. By the end of the war, Russia had lost 107 boats to enemy action and accidents.

Regent, an 'R' class boat, departing from Malta. Intended, like the 'O' and 'P' classes, for use in the Far East, these boats were really too big for the confined waters of the Mediterranean but had to be used until the new boats from the wartime construction programmes became available.

An early 'U' class boat at Malta, c.1941. The original caption claims it to be the famous Upholder. Commanded by the leading British ace, David Wanklyn VC, Upholder sank 135,000 tons of Axis shipping in twelve months. On what should have been their last patrol before a long-overdue rest, Wanklyn and his boat were lost off Tripoli during a convoy attack in April 1942.

An Italian tanker burns. Tankers were priority targets but, as their cargo provided additional buoyancy, they were difficult to sink if they failed to catch fire.

Unruly of the 10th Flotilla, Manoel Island, Malta, in March 1945. Their small size and twenty second diving time made the 'U' class ideal boats for the shallow coastal waters of the Mediterranean. The damaged buildings in the background show the effects of the constant bombing by the Regia Aeronautica and Luftwaffe; the air raids were so intense that submarines had to sit on the harbour bottom during daylight, surfacing only under cover of darkness. It was hardly the best place for a rest after an arduous war patrol.

Safari coming alongside the depot ship HMS Forth in Holy Loch on her return from the Mediterranean on 19 September 1943. From her periscope top a 'Jolly Roger' is flying, indicating a successful patrol. Horton had first flown the pirate's flag in 1914, much to Their Lordship's displeasure, and the habit was revived in the Second World War by the 10th Flotilla at Malta. It became a popular custom.

Safari's CO, 'Ben' Bryant, was an enthusiastic advocate of the deck gun. Faced with an increasing shortage of large merchant ships, the enemy resorted to using small vessels to move their supplies, hugging the coastline for protection. Too small to waste a valuable torpedo on, Bryant would surface and sink them with gunfire, often close inshore under the nose of the enemy defences. Alastair Mars in *Unbroken* surfaced off Calabria and gunned a train. Similar conditions existed in the Far East where the US Navy had wiped out the Japanese merchant fleet. In the absence of anything more substantial, British boats had to go after small coasters and junks but were faced with a moral dilemma as many were manned by press-ganged crews from Japan's conquered territories. If the situation permitted, crews were transferred to an undamaged vessel and allowed to go on their way, and any who wanted to join the Allies were taken on board the submarine.

The British were not totally alone in the Mediterranean theatre. Alongside them fought the Polish Sokol and several boats from the Dutch and Royal Hellenic navies. This is the Greek Glavcos entering Malta. She was sunk there by bombs on 4 April 1942.

HMS P-556, formerly S29 of the US Navy, after transfer in 1942 to the Royal Navy who used her for training duties. Originally designed for the Atlantic, the 'S' boats were totally unsuited for operations in the Pacific, but they held the line for the Americans in the dark months after Japan attacked until more modern boats entered service.

Two 'T' boats alongside their depot ship. Some fifty-three 'T' class boats were built in three groups and, with a forward-firing salvo of ten torpedoes, they were the most powerful submarines in the world. They fought in the North Sea, Mediterranean, and the Far East, fifteen of them being lost in action. On the aft casing is the 138 ASDIC housing and the wire triangle is the radio direction finding aerial.

Seen here is the famous Tally-Ho. Under the command of Cmdr L.W.A. Bennington, she operated in the Malacca Strait from March 1943 to February 1945, sinking over 12,000 tons of Japanese shipping including the cruiser Kuma. She also survived having her port saddle tanks ripped open by the screws of an attacking torpedo boat.

U1023, *a Type VIIC, surrendered at Weymouth in May 1945. Her war service barely lasted a month, though she still managed to sink one ship. The tall vertical pipe in the foreground is the 'schnorkel' in its raised position, which allowed the boat to run on its diesel engines while submerged.*

U190, *a Type IX C/40, surrendered at St John's, Newfoundland in May 1945. Note the heavy anti-aircraft armament on the conning tower 'wintergartens' demonstrating how aircraft had become the major threat. In almost three years of active service, U190 sank only two ships.*

The Japanese heavy cruiser Ashigara at Spithead during the 1937 Coronation Review. On 8 June 1945, 'Baldy' Hezlet in Trenchant ambushed her off Banka Island. Hezlet had his victim trapped between the shore and a minefield and hit her with five torpedoes. Burning and waterlogged, but with her guns still firing at Trenchant's periscope, Ashigara rolled over and sank thirty minutes later.

The crippled Japanese heavy cruiser Takao in the Johore Strait. On 30 July 1945, the midget submarine XE3 penetrated the defences and placed explosive charges under Takao, almost becoming trapped under her target by the falling tide. The charges blew a sixty-foot hole in Takao's bottom, putting the ship permanently out of action. XE3's CO, Lt Fraser, and his diver 'Mike' Magennis were each awarded the Victoria Cross.

Launched in 1931, the minelayer Porpoise *had a successful, but ultimately tragic, career. She sank a U-boat off Egersund in April 1940. In the Mediterranean she ran 'Magic Carpet' supply runs to Malta and torpedoed a 10,000 ton tanker. She was sunk by the Japanese off Penang in January 1945, the last British submarine to be lost in the war. The chances of survival for a British submariner were even, and the final reckoning was grim: 75 boats lost, 3,142 men killed.*

'A' class boats fitting out at Vickers-Armstrong's Barrow yard in 1945.

'T' boats of the 4th Flotilla alongside the depot ship HMS Adamant at Sydney in 1945.

Alliance with attack and search periscopes up and her 'snort' (snorkel) raised. With a range of 10,000 miles, the 'A's were specifically designed for operations against the Japanese, although none were ready before the war ended. Rebuilt and modernised in the late 1950s, most continued in service until the early 1970s. Alliance is now preserved as a walk-through exhibit at the RN Submarine Museum, Gosport.

Tigerhaai (ex- HMS Tarn) at Rotterdam with a Sikorsky S55 winching off a crewman. There is a symbiotic love/hate relationship between the submarine and the helicopter: the latter can be an ally, ideal for providing support, but with its dipping sonar and homing torpedoes, also a deadly foe.

Five

Today and Tomorrow

The application of nuclear power to submarines changed everything. Freed from the necessity of rising to the surface to recharge batteries and replenish the air, nuclear power conferred on submarines unlimited underwater range, high speed and endurance. When the USS *Nautilus* first put to sea in 1955 she sailed into a world riven by mutual distrust and paranoia, both America and Russia believing each was hell-bent on overthrowing the other. With the proliferation of nuclear weapons and the fear of pre-emptive nuclear attacks, both the USA and the Soviet Union came to regard the ballistic missile-carrying submarine (SSBN) as their only absolute guarantee of being able to launch a retaliatory strike. As Russia lacked both long-range missiles and strategic bombers, Admiral Gorshkov shifted the Soviet Navy from a primarily coastal defence force into a blue water navy, with its submarines the spearhead. Both conventional diesel and nuclear-powered boats would stalk US and NATO battle groups, interdict the sea-lanes and hunt the capitalist's submarines, while ballistic missile boats would lurk threateningly off the North American coast. The US Navy's response was to tail closely every Soviet 'boomer' with a hunter-killer boat, beginning a dangerous game of cat-and-mouse that lasted throughout the Cold War, and probably still goes on, spread across the oceans of the globe.

Teredo *alongside the carrier* Albion, *c.1957, with her 'snort' half-raised. Many of the 'T's were rebuilt post-war as fast streamlined hunter-killers, remaining in service until the late 1960's. Despite their outstanding war record, none were preserved.*

Once Russian submariners realised they were being followed they developed a tactic to clear their baffles, checking the sonar blind spot astern created by the acoustics from their own propellers. Making a sudden 180 degree turn, they came charging back on a reciprocal heading. American submariners called the manoeuvre a 'Crazy Ivan' and, though always officially denied, the occasional bump inevitably occurred. The constant shadowing forced the Soviets to withdraw many of their SSBNs into heavily defended bastions in the Sea of Okhotsk, the Barents Sea and the Arctic Ocean. The polar ice cap was a good place to hide submarines. They were protected from satellite surveillance and the environment of icebergs, causing variations in heat and density, made sonar conditions horrendous for any prowling attack boat. American boats operating in the Arctic had a further, unexpected, problem to contend with. Their active sonar gave off sounds similar to the mating calls of the local seal population. No amorous encounters were recorded and, given the size disparity, it would have been a love unrequited, but the 'pingers' were probably grateful their equipment did not sound like a lovesick blue whale.

Britain joined the nuclear boat club in 1960 with the launch of HMS *Dreadnought*. Yet there is a downside to the new technology. The power plants generate a lot of noise, particularly at high speed, and the size of the boats creates a large sonar footprint. There is also the long-term problem of safely disposing of the highly radioactive cores when the boats are retired from service.

Nuclear-powered USS Triton *leaving Portsmouth on 10 July 1964. Completed in 1959,* Triton *was unique. Designed as a radar picket to provide extended cover for a surface battle group,* Triton *needed two reactors to produce the necessary high surface speed. As a result, she was the largest submarine yet built. Improved radar technology made* Triton *irrelevant and she was laid up after less than ten years service.*

In tandem with the application of nuclear power to submarines came the application of nuclear missiles. With the ratification of an agreement between the US and Britain in 1962, the former agreed to sell the UK Polaris missiles, which would carry British-produced warheads. Britain's 'independent' nuclear deterrent was – and still is – a contentious issue, some arguing the policy to be less about defence than about maintaining global prestige: 'Rule Britannia' posturing as political influence and economic power declines. Or, as one Royal Navy officer saw it, 'putting hairs on chests'. As Britain is a member of NATO and sheltered by the American nuclear umbrella, it can be argued that the large chunks of defence budgets spent on Polaris and then Trident might have been more wisely used on other areas, without the Royal Navy suffering shortfalls in capability.

Unexpectedly, the Royal Navy was again pushed into war. For many years the Royal Air Force had been conducting a covert propaganda campaign in the corridors of Whitehall, convincing both civil servants and politicians that Britain's overseas interests could be adequately protected by land-based air power alone. The net result had been a steady erosion of naval capability since the late 1950s and the Conservative Government was planning further drastic cuts in 1982. When Argentina seized the Falkland Islands that same year it was proved, yet again, that only a navy has the reach and equipment to launch an effective and measured long-distance response.

British submarines played a significant part in the campaign, though, with one notable exception, generally low-key. Their principal role was the enforcement of the Exclusion Zone around the islands and this led to the last dramatic submarine versus surface ship engagement of the century. On 2 May, the hunter-killer *Conqueror* hit the *General Belgrano* with a torpedo. Not with one of the new wire-guided Tigerfish, developed at vast expense and with numerous political photo opportunities, but a MK8 of the Second World War vintage. Its target was a cruiser that dated from the same war, a ship designed to survive just such an attack. Consequently, the *Belgrano* stayed afloat for some time. When she finally sank she took 350 young men with her, and the Argentine Navy did not venture near the islands again. It was a powerful reminder of the submarine's ability to deny others the use of the sea, reminiscent of those early days when Boyle and Nasmith crept into the Marmara, and Hersing's U-boat caused panic off the Dardanelles. The wheel had come full circle.

What then of the future? With the collapse of the Soviet Union, the focus of naval planning has shifted from global to regional, from blue water to the littoral. But, despite the increasing sophistication of ASW systems the submarine still holds the initiative, and assets that might otherwise be deployed in offensive operations are tied down in defensive anti-submarine positions. The underwater threat still generates anxiety and has the potential to inhibit surface operations. Argentine submarines during the Falkland War, and a possible Iraqi boat in the Straits of Hormuz during the Gulf War, were sources of major concern. That neither threat actually materialised is beside the point. It is the credibility of the threat that matters.

Contemporary defence analysis tends to be predicated along linear paths, yet the nature of armed conflict has changed, making it difficult to anticipate the unpredictable, the erratic actions of the embittered terrorist or would-be messiah, and still more difficult to counter such threats with conventional weapons. All that can be said with any certainty is that if the human race continues to use the sea when fighting its wars, the submarine will remain a key weapon. And in the first year of the new century, the loss of the Russian *Kursk* and its fine crew is a depressing reminder that, for the submariner, some things have not changed at all.

A ' Porpoise' class hunter-killer in a beam sea. It was a rough ride for the crew, but it helped negate the inherent positive buoyancy of the bows and thus speeded-up diving time. The 'Porpoise' class was the first new post-war British design and it led directly to the excellent 'Oberon' class of the 1960s, which remained in service into the early 1990s.

The USS Tunny launching a Regulus surface-to-surface missile in the Central Pacific in November 1955. As submarines are most vulnerable when surfaced and as the Regulus took some time to prepare and launch, this was more a proof-of-concept than a viable weapon system but it became the forerunner of today's lethal sub-surface launched weapons such as Harpoon. Official US Navy photograph.

Queen Elizabeth II launching the Royal Navy's first nuclear-powered submarine, HMS Dreadnought, at Vickers-Armstrong's Barrow yard on 21 October 1960.

A defining moment for the Submarine Service. Dreadnought goes down the ways.

Dreadnought returning from sea trials on 13 December 1962. She remained in service until 1982. Nuclear-powered submarines are of unlimited range and capable of remaining submerged indefinitely. Endurance is only limited by the finite supply of food, and the stamina of the crews.

Courageous, a 'Valiant' class nuclear-powered attack boat (SSN) shortly after completion in May 1971. Developed from Dreadnought and forerunner of the 'Swiftsure' and 'Trafalgar' classes, these SSNs provided much useful operational experience. They also went to war: the Courageous was on station during the Falkland War and her sister, the Conqueror, sank the Belgrano.

A 'Resolution' class SSBN from the 10th Squadron, based at Faslane. With sixteen Polaris missiles apiece, the four boats of this class carried Britain's strategic nuclear deterrent from the end of the 1960s until replaced by the Trident missile 'Vanguard' class in 1996. One boat was always at sea on a three month patrol somewhere in the world, its position a closely guarded secret to everyone except, probably, the Russians.

The USS Blueback, a 'Barbel' class patrol submarine at Hong Kong in September 1970. Conventional diesel-electric boats, the 'Barbel's fell victim to the all-nuclear school of thought that prevailed in the US. Many defence analysts consider this a mistake, believing conventional boats still have a useful role to play in current naval operations.

Jettisoning its protective nose cap, a Sub-Harpoon breaks surface, booster motor igniting automatically. Launched from a standard torpedo tube, Sub-Harpoon is an all-weather, over-the-horizon, sea-skimming anti-ship missile that allows stand-off attacks against defended targets from ranges in excess of sixty-seven nautical miles. Under development is an upgrade with a global positioning and inertial navigation system enabling precision strikes against land or harbour targets. Of much greater range is the Tomahawk cruise missile, fired for the first time by HMS Splendid during the Kosovo crisis. Trafalgar, Triumph and Spartan are being modified to carry this missile.

HMS Torbay, a 'Trafalgar' class SSN on her sea trials in 1986. On the casing is the retractable sonar housing and the hull is very smooth to reduce flow noise. It is also coated with anechoic tiles both to suppress internal noises and absorb incoming active sonar 'pings', and the machinery is insulated and damped to further reduce the acoustic signature. Armed with wire-guided Spearfish torpedoes and Sub-Harpoons, with a submerged speed of thirty-plus knots and an operational depth in excess of 1,000 feet, these are fearsome hunter-killers. Photo courtesy of BAE SYSTEMS

A 'Lira' class SSN of the Soviet Navy. Codenamed 'Alfa' by NATO, their arrival in the late 1970s caused much consternation in the West, though Naval Intelligence regularly overestimated the capabilities of Soviet submarines. Whether this was due simply to poor analysis, some considering the concept of military intelligence in general an oxymoron, or intended to panic politicians and budget planners into spending more on defence, depends on one's degree of scepticism. Soviet submarines were not as technologically sophisticated as their American or British equivalents, Russian nuclear boats being noisy and relatively easy to track, but their crews were a proud elite in a supposedly classless society, capable and brave with high morale.

The relatively small size of the 'Alfa's combined with the blended sail and titanium hull allowed for high underwater speed and manoeuvrability, and a maximum diving depth of 1,378 feet, but they were cramped to live in, difficult to repair, and their lead-bismuth liquid-metal reactors caused no end of trouble. All seven boats in the class had been retired by the mid-1990s.

Next Page;
A Russian 'Typhoon' SSBN in the Barents Sea being overflown by a Tupolev Tu-16 'Badger'. With an enormous displacement of 24,000 tons and carrying twenty ballistic missiles, the six boats of the 'Typhoon' class are the largest, most formidable, most intimidating submarines yet built, a symbol and a result of the mistrust and fear generated by the Cold War.

Carrying a proud name and heritage, this is Upholder, a diesel-electric attack submarine (SSK). Completed in 1989, Upholder was the name boat of the class. Of the nineteen boats originally planned, only four were built and they were mothballed in 1994 before being leased to Canada. Their retirement marked the final exit of diesel boats from the Royal Navy and with their departure went many of the sights and smells that caused such offence to traditional naval officers: oily waste, exhaust fumes, and grubby engine-room staff. Most of the things, in other words, that made submarines interesting. Photograph courtesy of BAE SYSTEMS.

An SSK of the Russian 'Varshavyanka' class. Codenamed 'Kilo' by NATO, the Project 877 Paltus boats are simple to operate, cheap to run and freely available on the export market. The prospect of one or more of these efficient and potentially deadly boats falling into the wrong hands is a constant source of anxiety to NATO and UN naval commanders.

A conventional Type S90 designed and built by Fincantieri of Italy. Although both the British and US submarine fleets are now all-nuclear many other navies prefer diesel-electric boats, believing them more suitable for littoral operations where the inherent quietness of the design helps them hide amongst the sonar-confusing 'reverberations' of shallow waters, thermal and salinity layers. Diesel-electric boats are also cheaper to purchase and their through-life operating costs are considerably lower. Neither are they quite so dependant on specialised – but vulnerable – fixed land bases. Recent problems with reactor cooling systems on the Royal Navy's 'Trafalgar' class have reinforced the faith of the diesel enthusiasts. Photograph courtesy of Fincantieri.

Opposite: An artist's impression of the future 'U214' class proposed by Howaldtswerke-Deutsche Werft. At first glance a conventional diesel boat, the '214' will have a fully integrated fuel cell system giving a continuous submerged endurance in excess of two weeks. With a faired, ferromagnetic hull and skew-back propeller to reduce hydrodynamic, magnetic and acoustic signatures, HDW claim the class will be virtually undetectable. Courtesy of HDW.

Twenty-first century boat. A computer generated image of Astute, the next generation SSN for the Royal Navy. This boat will dispense with conventional periscopes, relying instead on twin non-hull

penetrating optronic masts carrying thermal imaging, low-light and colour TV sensors. An electronic support measures (ESM) mast will also be included. Courtesy of BAE SYSTEMS.

127

With the threat becoming increasingly clever at avoiding detection, ASW platforms are becoming increasingly sophisticated at hunting it. Here, a Merlin, the latest in a long line of successful anti-submarine helicopters from Westland, hovers over a 'Swiftsure' SSN during ASW trials in the Bahamas in June 2000. One submarine CO was overheard saying he was thankful the Merlin's 'on our side'. Photograph courtesy of GKN Westland.

Survivors from Poseidon lay a wreath above the wreck of their boat on 14 June 1931. Let this image stand as a memorial to all the victims of undersea warfare: the submariners, the merchant sailors and the civilians, but especially the lost children of the Benares *and the* Wilhelm Gustloff.